DUNE COUNTRY

DUNE COUNTRY

A Hiker's Guide
to the Indiana Dunes

by GLENDA DANIEL

illustrations by CAROL LERNER

 SWALLOW PRESS
Athens

Revised edition, 1984

95 94 93 92 91 90   5 4 3 2

Cover drawing: Hop tree (wafer ash)

Swallow Press/Ohio University Press books
are printed on acid-free paper ⊛

Library of Congress Cataloging in Publication Data

Daniel, Glenda.
    Dune country.

    Includes index.
    1. Natural history—Indiana—Indiana Dunes National Lakeshore.
2. Indiana Dunes National Lakeshore (Ind.)—Guide-books. I. Title.
QH105.I6D363   1984   508.772'98   84-10366
ISBN 0-8040-0854-X (pbk.)

Contents

MAPS

Preface to the Revised Edition

A great deal has happened in the Indiana Dunes to change both natural and cultural history since the first edition of *Dune Country* was published; most of the change has, happily, been for the better.

Boundaries of the National Lakeshore, for instance, have been enlarged by Congressional authorization to more than 13,000 acres—almost double the size of the park when it was established in 1966. The new acquisitions include several prime natural areas, including a superlative oak savanna in Miller Woods, a section of what is now the park's West Unit where turn-of-the-century ecologist Henry Cowles did much of his early explorations. Many abandoned buildings have been torn down in the last few years, and native plants have begun to reassert themselves with a little help from the National Lakeshore science staff and volunteers.

Exceptions to the general improvement are the prairie remnants, which are badly in need of regular controlled burns, and increased erosion produced by the increase in human visitors. Indiana Dunes State Park has attracted close to a million visitors a year since the mid-1970s; by Labor Day 1983, more than 1.2 million had also visited the National Lakeshore.

A large cadre of professional naturalists—available for guided tours, film presentations, and visits to area schools and organizational meetings—has also developed at the Lakeshore since *Dune Country's* first edition. The state park, operating with more limited funds, has nonetheless also increased its staff of summer naturalists.

Because the book first appeared at the time these programs were getting underway, many of the new staff members used it to learn about the Dunes' natural history, to structure their talks and walks, and eventually, like all good students, to know more than their "teacher." The staffs are generous with their time and eager to answer visitors' questions as well as to offer tours.

The Save the Dunes Council, a strong group of volunteer dune supporters, protectors and watchers, has also continued to grow and thrive while the national park they helped to create grew to maturity around them. The organization made a prescient decision years ago not to disband when the National Lakeshore was established. As a result they have been able to lobby consistently and effectively over the years for each new piece of desired ground, each new facility and program.

This new edition of *Dune Country* hasn't changed much, for all that, except for an expanded geology section, the addition of several new trails, a much-needed index, and corrections pointed out by conscientious readers. Acknowledgment for corrections is due, in particular, to Emma Pitcher of Chesterton.

The plants described in the first edition are still here; if anything they are even more firmly entrenched now. Many readers have asked why we failed to include a number of wildflowers and other plants which are common at the Dunes. Two examples among many such plants are the common buttercup, a native, and the purple flowering loosestrife, an exotic. Our answer is that the area is unusually rich and diverse in its plant collections, and we couldn't have begun, in a volume of this size and scope, to include all of the common species. We narrowed our focus deliberately, for that reason, to the plants we felt were particularly indicative of dune habitats, not only here but throughout the Great Lakes and, to some extent, in sandy coastal regions as well. Perhaps some of you will write the remaining books which are needed to tell the whole Dunes story.

May 1984   GLENDA DANIEL
                                                      CAROL LERNER

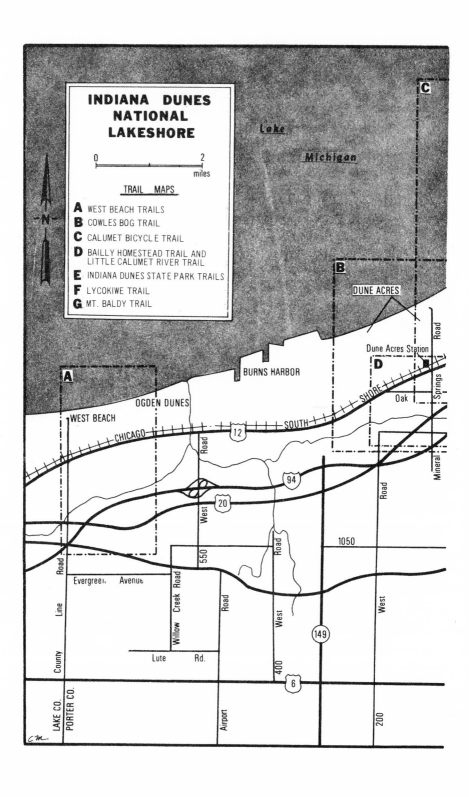

INDIANA DUNES
NATIONAL
LAKESHORE

0 ———————— 2
miles

TRAIL MAPS

A WEST BEACH TRAILS
B COWLES BOG TRAIL
C CALUMET BICYCLE TRAIL
D BAILLY HOMESTEAD TRAIL AND
  LITTLE CALUMET RIVER TRAIL
E INDIANA DUNES STATE PARK TRAILS
F LYCOKIWE TRAIL
G MT. BALDY TRAIL

—N—

Lake
Michigan

DUNE ACRES

Dune Acres Station

BURNS HARBOR

OGDEN DUNES

WEST BEACH

CHICAGO

SOUTH SHORE

Oak

12

94

20

West Road

550

Willow Creek Road

Evergreen Avenue

Lute Rd.

Road

1050

149

400

6

West

200

Airport

Mineral Road

Springs Road

County Line Road

LAKE CO.
PORTER CO.

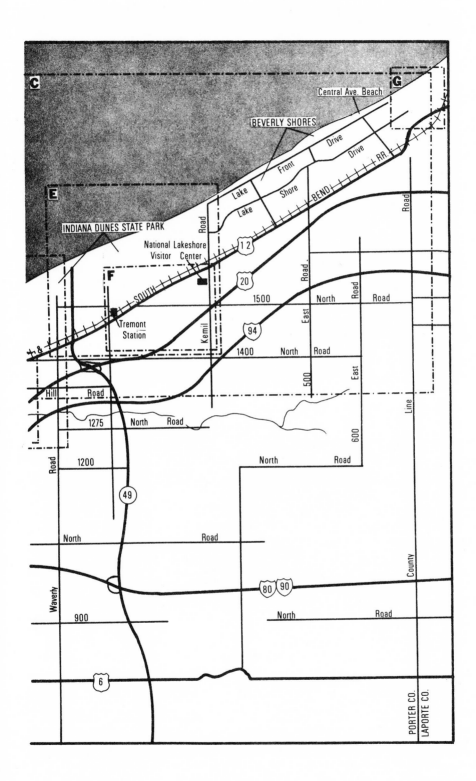

Introduction

Indiana dune country stretches along Lake Michigan's southern shore across fourteen miles of windswept beach between
the cities of Gary and Michigan City. Inland for a mile and a
half, it climbs over the high, grass-tussocked sand hills which
give the place its name, dips down through cool pine forests,
marshes, and tamarack bogs, into ancient oak woodlands on
gentle ridges where acorns have dropped and blueberries have
ripened on the ground for thousands of years.

Our country's first urban national park, the dune country
is hemmed in today by houses, factories and highways, a
patchwork refuge of some 12,000 wild acres in the heart of

1

America's industrial Midwest. Before the twentieth century, it was largely uninhabited. Until the nineteenth century not even many of the region's native Potawatomie Indians had ventured to linger overnight. They came in the cool of the morning to hunt quail or harvest blueberries and left before darkness fell. Early trappers plied the Little Calumet River, cursed the mosquitoes, and hurried away with their furs.

John Tipton, a surveyor for the state of Indiana, predicted in the early 1800s that the dunes area with its ponds and marshes and sand hills "can never admit of settlement nor never will be of much service to our state."

He reckoned without the curiosity of scientists, men like Henry Chandler Cowles and Victor Shelford from the nearby Universities of Chicago and Illinois, who found in the unique landscape a perfect natural laboratory for understanding how communities of plants and animals evolve, how a hill of sand where only the hardiest of grasses can grow may eventually become rich enough to support a forest of oaks. Their studies laid the groundwork for the modern science of ecology.

Tipton also reckoned without the insight of Judge Elbert Gary, an ambitious young lawyer from Wheaton, Illinois, who saw in the flat sandy shores the perfect place to dredge a harbor for the needs of a new industrial age. He built a vast steel mill in the dunes and a city in the sands. He named the city for himself and invited workers in his plant to come and make their homes there.

The surveyor, the trappers, and the Indians would have found it hard to imagine the appeal of summer homes on the dunes or the pilgrimages of city dwellers looking in a forest of concrete for a few green plants with which to remember wilderness, a place to walk on bare earth, to sleep under stars.

The earliest visitors to the area were too busy unmiring their oxen and wagons from the shoulder-deep mud of the marshes to notice the great variety of wildflowers growing there. Prickly pear cactus, a plant of desert habits, nestled on the dunes unremarked next to eastern woodland plants like trillium and boreal flowers like pipsissewa and bearberry, the latter two lingering from the time when a glacier still hovered just offshore.

It was the glacier which gave the area both its special appeal and its disadvantages, depending on whose eyes are surveying the landscape. The marshes and bogs where the pioneer wagons mired down are its after-effects. So are the hills of sand where Gary built his mill and the scientists made their discoveries about how plant communities evolve. On the ground, the dune country seems at first like a hopeless confusion of hills and valleys, sloping off in all directions to mislead unwary hikers. From the air, a pattern emerges in the landscape. Long low ridges, each with its complex of dunes and each major one separated by a narrow ribbon of marshland, run east to west, paralleling the lakeshore. At least three of the main ridges were once shorelines themselves. The oldest and gentlest, where gnarled black oaks and high-crowned maples grow now, dates from a time when the lake stood some sixty feet higher than its current elevation. Between that old shore and the present one are the records, in kinds of plant and animal life, of some fourteen thousand years of landscape evolution, spread bizarrely over space instead of time. It was these old beach ridges that made such a great laboratory for Cowles and Shelford, and their existence is one of the reasons people have fought long and hard to save the dunes from further development in the form of homes and factories.

Efforts began as early as 1909 when members of the Prairie Club of Chicago began propagandizing legislators and other influential citizens by taking them on hikes through the dunes. In 1916 a Gary chapter of the Daughters of the American Revolution planted a flag on Mount Tom, highest of the dunes, and declared, in the fashion of Balboa surveying the Pacific, that the lands henceforth belonged to the people and should be made a national park. It was to take more than speeches and flag planting. Stephen Mather, first director of the National Park Service, held hearings on the national lakeshore proposal in 1916, but it was the state of Indiana which acted first to save the dunes with a state park of 2,200 acres established in 1923.

Conservationists, working in recent years through a coalition of groups and individuals called the Save the Dunes Council, toiled four long decades more before the National Lakeshore became a reality in 1966. Congressional legislation that year, spearheaded by the late Senator Paul Douglas of Chicago, authorized purchase of more than six thousand additional acres. The state park acreage was included within the new national park boundaries at its dedication in 1972 but continues to be administered separately by the state of Indiana. In 1976 a bill was passed by Congress and signed by President Gerald Ford authorizing purchase of nearly thirty-seven hundred more acres.

Half a century has passed now since those early dune lovers raised the flag on Mount Tom. Thanks to their efforts and those of their modern counterparts, we have a chance today to see and explore the same sort of landscape that excited or daunted our ancestors. We can lie on a sunlit beach and imagine the scraping of early trappers' canoes on the sand. We can pick blueberries where the Potawatomies foraged. We can camp on the same ridges where pioneer wagons rolled, mosquito-netted tents our only concession to modernity. And we can play at ecological detective if we like, in the manner of Dr. Cowles. We wrote this book, in fact, because we believe current dune visitors are as curious to understand what they see as the early scientists were.

We have an advantage over Dr. Cowles, of course. Thanks to his work and that of his followers, we know now how the hardy clumps of marram grass build mountains of sand and how the sand can eventually become rich enough to support prairies or giant oak forests.

We know that junipers and pines grow on windward slopes while basswoods thrive best on the sheltered lee sides of dunes and that the tiny tiger beetles that scurry along the driftwood of the shore are entirely different species from those found only hundreds of yards away in the shade of the pines.

We know where to go for a trip through time in half an hour's stroll. All we have to do along the way is open our eyes and see.

GEOLOGY

In the beginning was the glacier Wisconsinan, last of the four great ice sheets to blanket the Midwest. A mile thick and more than four million square miles in extent, it stretched once from Hudson Bay almost to the banks of the Ohio River. The rolling hills of sand, the tangled marshes, prairie, and forest of today's Indiana Dunes were created entirely since that glacier began to recede, melting from the area some fourteen thousand years ago to form Lake Chicago, prehistoric ancestor to Lake Michigan.

An advancing glacier scours the ground, grinding bedrock to powder and impartially snatching up grains of sand and boul-

ders the size of basketballs. A melting glacier releases all this
stuff, in great hills of debris at the ice front and in long trains
carried away from the ice by the rush of meltwater. A stationary
ice front, a glacier whose annual advance just about equals its
annual melt, is continuously conveying new debris forward to
be dropped at the melting edge—which never moves. The hills
of glacial drift grow ever higher, the depressions between them
ever deeper. The landscapes of knobby hills and kettle-shaped
valleys the ice creates are called *moraines.*

The biggest moraine in dune country is the Valparaiso, which
is visible from the highest lakeshore dunes as a range of hills on
the southern horizon. The ice must have long remained at the
Valparaiso Moraine. Its highest hills are nearly 900 feet above
sea level and more than 200 feet above Lake Michigan. It surrounds the southern end of the lake, forming the Palos Hills in
Illinois southwest of Chicago and creating a cluster of lakes that
extends north from Palos to Wisconsin. Here in Indiana it is the
divide between the Great Lakes and the Mississippi. Rain fall-
ing on the south slope of the moraine flows south to the Kankakee and the Illinois; the north slopes lead down to the lake.

All of the state and national parkland in the dunes lies north
of the Valparaiso Moraine except Pinhook Bog, an isolated par-
cel of the National Lakeshore that lies in the moraine south of
Michigan City. Pinhook began when a huge block of ice calved
from the face of the glacier and fell into the debris of the moraine. When the ice block melted, it left a water-filled depression that in time evolved into the bog. Most lakes on moraines
have a similar history.

The Valparaiso Moraine dates from a relatively warm period
16,000 to 14,000 years ago. At the end of that time the ice retreated northward, only to advance again and lay down the
Tinley Moraine. This feature lies directly atop the north slope
of the Valparaiso Moraine. Its existence was discovered by dig-
ging into the ground and noting changes in the composition of
glacial deposits. On the surface it is impossible to separate the
Tinley and Valparaiso Moraines.

A third morainic system, the Lake Border Moraine, dates
from the last advance of the ice out of what is now the Lake

Michigan Basin. The Lake Border Moraine is visible as an area of high ground comprising the Tremont area of the National Lakeshore.

The same rocks and soil that piled up to make the moraine are strung out in long *outwash plains* beneath the sands and marshes of the dunes. Moraines are a great jumble of debris, but outwash usually has a more sorted look. In the first rush of water from the ice, even boulders could be shoved along by the torrent. But as the water spread out and slowed down, the bigger stones would fall first, followed by the pebbles, grains of sand and silt, and finally the tiny particles of clay. The extent of sorting on the outwash plains of the dunes is unknown, as most of this ground is deeply buried under thousands of years' worth of drifting sand. We can see fragments of it in sand-mined areas inland or in the outwash pebbles on the modern beach. They make up a kind of museum, with samples of mineral-rich boulders and bits of gravel in every sort of texture and color— carried south with the ice from all over eastern Canada and the northern United States. To find bedrock, pressed layers of gray-green shale with its fossil evidence of life before the Ice Age, one would have to dig through the sand and underlying clay, through the museum of Ice Age rocks—down at least 140 feet, and in some places more than 250 feet below the surface.

The first Great Lake was born here about 14,000 years ago when the ice was retreating from the Tinley and Lake Border Moraines. Dammed between the ice front and the hills of Valparaiso, the chilly waters deepened as the ice melted away. This was Lake Chicago, ancestor of Lake Michigan. For a time it stabilized at 640 feet above sea level, about 60 feet above the contemporary shore of Lake Michigan. The beat of the waves and the endless winds created a ridge of sand, a beach that marks the ancient shore. Lakeward from the beach, offshore sand bars enclosed ancient lagoons.

This was the Glenwood Stage of Lake Chicago, the oldest, and therefore southernmost, of the three lake stages whose traces are visible in dune country. Most of the sand ridge marking the old beach is on the flank of the Valparaiso Moraine, south of the dunes. The lagoons are now wetlands. The Glenwood shore does enter the National Lakeshore boundaries in the Tremont-Furnessville area where it forms a belt of low wooded sandhills between U.S. Highways 20 and 12 from the Bailly Cemetery west of Dune Acres to park headquarters at Kemil Road. Lake Chicago remained at the Glenwood beach stage until the melting water rose high enough to spill over the earth and boulder dike of the moraine in the Palos Hills southwest of Chicago. The gap in the moraine there made the Des Plaines River the outlet for the young Great Lakes. Today the Des Plaines is a muddy little stream. Then, it was a mile-wide torrent, milky with rock flour like Alaskan Rivers of today. The sheer volume of water and glacial outwash pouring through the loose material of the moraine at Palos quickly cut the channel of the Des Plaines from 640 feet above sea level to 620 feet. But at that level, the river ran into a dam of huge boulders that for a time resisted the rushing waters. The shores of Lake Chicago stabilized again at the Calumet stage. The Calumet Beach Ridge is a prominent feature of the Dunes. It was a highway from earliest times, and in the twentieth century it provided a high, dry route for U.S. 12 through the dunes. The extensive wetlands north of the highway, including Long Lake in the West Beach Unit and the Cowles Bog area south of Dune Acres, were lagoons in Calumet time.

About 11,000 years ago, the Des Plaines broke the boulder dam and scoured its channel down to bedrock. Lake Chicago dropped again to stabilize at the Tolleston Stage, just 25 feet above the present lake level. Today, beach dunes of Tolleston age overlap both Calumet sands and more recent creations. However, the Inland Marsh area south of Route 12 in the West Beach Unit of the National Lakeshore shows dunes of Tolleston age.

It's hard to tell in most places just where the Tolleston beach dunes end and those of present-day Lake Michigan begin. It has been 2,000 years, after all, since the lake—after many fluctuations—reached its present level of between 575 and 585 feet above sea level. That happened after the ice had completely left the Great Lakes Basin and after crustal rebound—the slow rising of the earth's crust once it was free of the weight of the ice

—had closed an outlet through North Bay, Ontario. Today, the Des Plaines River is no longer in the Great Lakes watershed and the flow of water from Lake Michigan is north through the Straits of Mackinac to Lake Huron.

The glacier has long since disappeared from eastern North America, but many of the other forces that shaped the ancient beach ridges continue to affect Indiana Dunes today. Prevailing winds still come from the Northwest in winter, bringing new supplies of sand scoured from the lake's bottom or eroded from steep banks on Wisconsin and Illinois shores. Rainfall and evaporation still vary from year to year, and barometric pressure alternates from high to low, sloshing the lake from side to side like water in a bathtub.

Sandbars still pile up offshore, too, catching sand that winter storms take from the beach, sending it landward again on the gentle breezes of summer. When it reaches the shore, the sand moves inland as it has always moved, rolling along gently in light breezes, colliding in rougher winds to form a chain reaction called saltation. As each grain hits another, the second one bounces into the air in a high, arching curve. When it lands, it jars more grains loose and the process continues. If you look at wet beach sand through a microscope, you will notice that its edges are smooth, polished by the water. But the sand in the high dunes has many rough edges, a result of the battering it has taken in saltation. Miniature ripples of the bouncing balls of sand edge upward along the beach when winds are high enough to crease the sand's surface. The patterns they make, gentle on the lake side, steeper to leeward, are repeated on a giant scale in the shapes of dunes themselves.

The dunes of deserts like the Sahara are formed entirely from ripples, little ones catching up to and merging with bigger ones until the whole mass of shifting sand, like a giant snowball, lumbers to a halt from sheer bulk.

Dunes in Indiana, with the lake at their back, are much more fertile and more complex than the dunes of the Sahara, however. Their shape and texture and size are determined by the sun and the wind but also by an abundance of plant life.

THE BEACH

The beach at Indiana Dunes State Park on a hot summer day is crowded with swimmers and sunbathers, frisbee tossers and volleyball players. The scene is much the same on the National Lakeshore beaches. Visitors mix their doses of sand, sun, and country air with tanning oil and hampers of sandwiches—at West Beach near Gary, at the ends of State Park Road and Central Avenue in Beverly Shores, and at Mount Baldy on Rice Street near Michigan City.

Each of these shores is also crowded with another, less obvious kind of life, that of native dune dwellers whose births, deaths, and daily routines over centuries have combined with wind, weather, and lake currents to create the landscape the human guests are there to enjoy.

This life begins at the margin of the lake, where the remains of fish, birds, and insects washed ashore by the waves provide food for a host of creatures. Among them are the scavengers, varying in size and taste preferences from the tiny carrion flies who dine delicately on microscopic maggots to ring-billed gulls and herring gulls, whose idea of a gourmet meal may be a ten-pound salmon.

Mammals like skunks and raccoons come down to the water's edge too, but, shyer, they wait until dark, content to feast on leftovers of meals the bolder animals began.

Fragile-legged shorebirds—sanderlings and spotted sandpipers, dunlins and ruddy turnstones—arrive to pick at the scavenging insects and look for crustaceans. They are joined by other predators, robber flies, and two species (white and copper) of tiger beetles, the insects that so fascinated zoologist Victor Shelford. He discovered early in this century that every special habitat in dune country, be it pond or swamp, open dune or pine forest, nourishes its own particular brand of tiger beetle, the territory of each marked with precise "no trespassing" signs —invisible to the curious eyes of people but apparently obvious to other tiger beetles. From his discoveries, Shelford drew his by now classic theories of animal succession to match what Dr. Cowles had already learned about plants.

Human visitors who try scraping bare toes along the band of wet beach just above the water's edge may make a scientific discovery of their own—very different from Shelford's observation of tiger beetles but just as startling in its way. Friction from a special combination of quartz crystals and moisture, activated by pressure from a person's hand or foot, produces a kind of music, a high, clear ringing tone, a natural tuning fork. Moist bands of a few other very special beaches around the world are known to produce tones of exactly the same pitch.

The constant wash of waves on this lower section of beach makes it impossible for plants to survive; but on the middle beach, that part of the sandy expanse touched by waves only in summer storms, a few hardy specimens of greenery take hold, blossom, grow, and die before winter. They are called annuals because they must start new from seed every spring. The first one you're likely to see on a beach at Indiana Dunes is the sea rocket. A succulent member of the mustard family, the sea rocket has fleshy stems that hold water and glossy leaves that feel cool to the touch on the hottest summer day. The sea rocket's stem and leaf construction, along with that of its sturdy roots, are the special adaptations that make its life possible on such a harsh frontier. It has tiny white or pale purple flowers in summer, double-jointed seed pods among its yellowing leaves in autumn.

Not far from the sea rocket, or maybe even huddling beside it, sharing protection against the wind's force from a piece of driftwood, are more native beach dwellers. None of the plants have beautiful names. Bugseed. Cocklebur. Winged pigweed and seaside spurge. Beauty is not a quality required or much revered on frontiers.

The bugseed is a stiff, many-branched plant with narrow, pointed leaves that bare as little surface as possible to the heat of the sun. By the time its flowers appear, green, solitary, inconspicuous, the leaves, no longer needed to change sunlight into food, begin to fall. Its seeds, tucked into bracts, grow in erect spikes. When the plant dies in autumn and its roots lose their tenuos grasp on the sand, it may be seen rolling along the beach. Bugseed is also known locally as tumbleweed.

The Russian thistle, introduced from Asia, is also common on Indiana Dunes beaches as well as on sandy and cindery disturbed areas throughout the area. It belongs to the same family as bugseed and looks very similar to it. It is shrubby and many-branched with sharp prickly leaves. Its stem is purplish striped, and tiny purple flowers bloom in September in its leaf axils.

The cocklebur of the dunes is the same one you see in vacant lots in a city. Its leaves are wide with a coarse, scratchy texture

Bugseed   Sea-rocket

Russian thistle

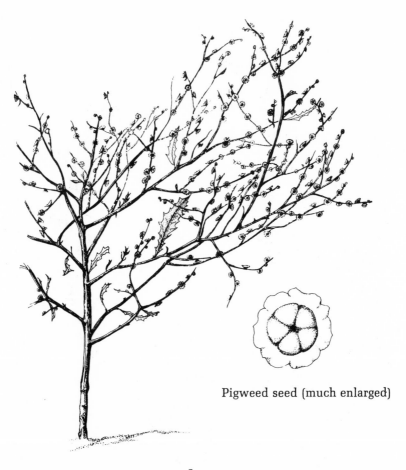

Pigweed seed (much enlarged)

Winged pigweed

that holds moisture as effectively as the fleshy leaves of the sea rocket. Its fruits are the big brown burs that attach themselves to your clothes when you brush by.

Winged pigweed has sharp-pointed leaves that look like miniature Christmas holly. Late in the season, when its wiry branchlets have turned purple and most of the leaves have fallen, it can still be spotted by the round winged fruits for which it was named.

Seaside spurge protects itself from wind by growing prostrate along the ground. Its stems have a milky juice and its tiny leaves, growing opposite each other, are long and narrow. It branches again and again as it grows, making an everwidening mat over the surface of the sand.

There are animals on the middle beach, too, burrowing into cool layers of sand beneath the surface or hiding under drift-

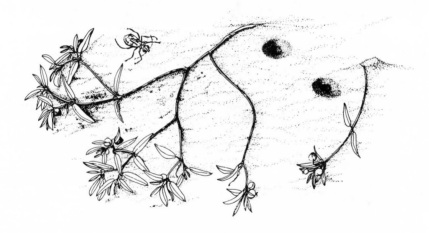

Seaside spurge. The insect is a mature white tiger beetle, and the holes are burrows of its larvae.

Fowler's toad   Cocklebur

wood. Fowler's toads are there, along with an occasional white-footed or deer mouse, a few burrowing spiders, and the sand-colored spider, special to the dunes. Various kinds of predatory beetles explore the decaying debris for a meal among colonies of white ants and termites, and long, raised tunnels in the sand testify to the presence of moles. Ladybird beetles collect in great numbers on the plants of the middle beach for autumn's mating season.

Temporary and tiny sand dunes may form in summer around the driftwood and the sea rocket or seaside spurge. No dunes of any size will appear, however, until the soil is rich enough and the ground far enough from pounding waves to make survival possible for perennials, plants that don't die in fall but continue to live from year to year.

To find a real dune at its moment of birth, one must search along the upper beach, beyond the reach of all but the worst of winter storms, for clumps of marram grass, probably the hardiest of all dune architects. Or you may stumble on a row of tiny cottonwood seedlings that sprouted in a once-damp depression, the kind left by a wheel mark or the print of human feet.

Near the grass and cottonwoods, it's possible to find a few more solitary outposts of dune life—wild rye and sand reed grass, a hairy puccoon or two, their yellow blossoms blinding in the intensity of their color.

It's hard to believe, watching these few plants nodding idly in the breeze, that they could have any major effect on a landscape. Yet a breathtaking view of their handiwork is but a few steps away—at the top of the first hill of sand.

FOREDUNES

Early on an August morning, before dew has dried from the grasses, the sunny open dunes behind the beach, called foredunes, are in their glory. Rolling hill after hill is crowded with plumes of goldenrod, the bright orange blossoms of butterfly weed, white-tipped bunches of horsemint. The stems of little bluestem prairie grass are actually maroon, but in late summer a spot at each joint on the stem becomes royal blue, not a color one expects to find in nature. The profusion seems random, without order at first. If you take a stroll inland, though, stepping gingerly among the flowers and grasses, you'll notice that

23

different groups of plants, like the animals that forage and build burrows in their shade, have special territories.

First come the real pioneers, the dune builders, plants that determine how wide and high, how steep or gentle the line of hills rising just behind the beach may grow to be. Marram grass and cottonwood trees are such pioneers. They are followed soon by sand cherry bushes, sand reed grasses, and fields of little bluestem. Flowers like horsemint and goldenrod, more strictly decorative in their contribution, are the last to appear, on dunes old enough and far enough from the lake to be protected from the wind's main force.

By late August, the marram grass has gone to seed, its compact flowering stalk a pale wheat color that makes a fine contrast with the still bright green of its narrow, pointed leaves. The seeds will lodge in sand all up and down the beach, but few of them will sprout. This particular grass spreads easiest —and in the process builds long, low, gently sloping dunes— by a method called *rhizome propagation*.

Rhizome is a Greek name for a special, dual-purpose kind of underground stem. As it probes down and then outward from its mother plant through moist layers of sand, the stem sprouts roots to drink more water, and it also sends fresh leafy shoots up to the surface to form new plants. One often sees rows of these tiny shoots on an upper beach at Indiana Dunes, marching along in single file like obedient soldiers.

The underground stem systems of marram grass eventually become vast networks, the rhizomes from a single plant spreading wide, sometimes as far as twenty feet, to hold in place the grains of sand captured by the above-ground grass blades. When high waves and wind wash the edge of a marram grass foredune away, this underground network is exposed, looking like a mat of uncombed hair or stuffing from an old sofa. If a piece of exposed rhizome breaks loose, it may be carried by winds along the beach to lodge and start a new colony of grasses, to build a new foredune, as much as a mile away.

A marram grass dune may eventually grow eight to ten feet

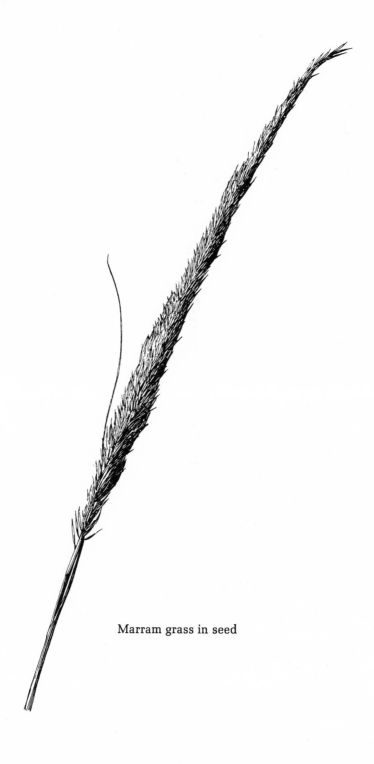

Marram grass in seed

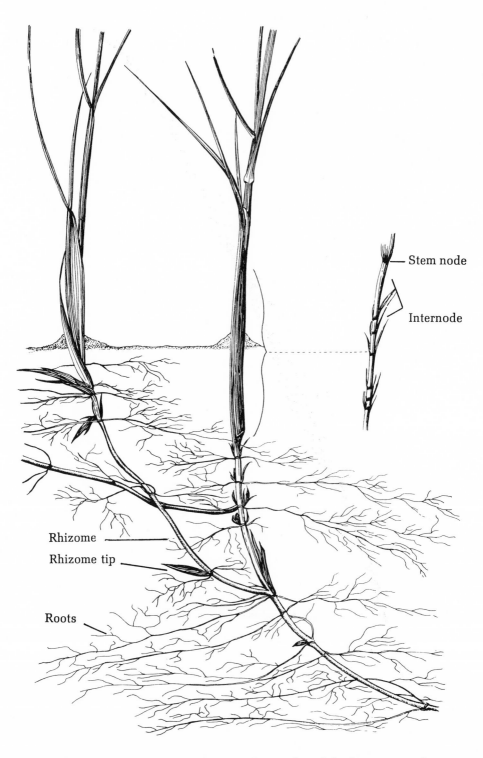

Stem node

Internode

Rhizome

Rhizome tip

Roots

Marram grass, showing underground growth and the lower part of the grass stem.

high because the plant's central stem, hidden entirely underground, keeps pushing the plant's leaves up for sun. It does
this by a special mechanism called *internodal elongation*. An
internode is the smooth section of stem between each joint,
and a marram grass plant may develop as many as a dozen
of these internodes in a year. If winds have been fierce and
sand has piled up rapidly during a particular year, the internodes will be long. If the dune has grown slowly, they will
be short and stubby. The plant makes a certain number of
them, however, even if a dune's growth slows drastically or
comes to a complete stop. When that happens, the internodes
push the stem above ground or so near the surface that moisture
is scarce, and the plant dies.

Cottonwood trees can also build dunes, steeper-sided in
their early stages than marram grass dunes because cottonwoods have no underground runners to extend their territory
sideways. Later, sand and wind blur the outlines of separate
foredunes, blending them into long, undulating ridges that
face the beach and lake. The gaunt forms of cottonwoods are
easy to recognize on these ridges because they're usually the
only kind of tree. Spaced widely between the rows of waving
grasses, they look like lonely sentinels on the ramparts of
some frontier fort.

Cottonwoods are seen most often along stream banks or at
the edge of marshes, and even in dry dune country they require sheltered, damp depressions in which to sprout. Once
they've gotten a good start, though, the same adaptations that
fit them for life in the wetlands make them good dune builders. They avoid both smothering by sand and drowning by
water because new roots can grow from the stems nearest
the surface when central trunk roots are buried dozens of
feet deep. What looks like a short, stubby cottonwood may
actually be only the exposed tip of a sixty-foot, hundred-year-
old tree.

The cottonwood's leaves are wide, almost triangular, and
coarsely toothed. In marshes or on streambanks farther in-

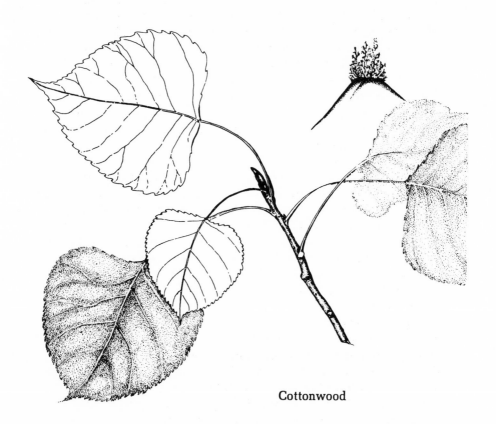

Cottonwood

land, it can be told from its relatives in the poplar family, big-toothed and quaking aspen, by two or more glands. Small but big enough to be seen without a magnifying glass, they are found on the head of its flat leafstalk where the stalk connects with the leaf blade. Cottonwood buds are reddish brown, sticky, and shiny.

When these plant pioneers on the first dune ridge catch a pile of sand high enough to block wind from the older dune behind it, the second dune becomes hospitable to tenants like little bluestem and sand reed grasses, along with stunted bushes of sand cherry.

Sand reed grass spreads by underground runners in much the same fashion as marram grass, but it is less successful at starting dunes nearest the beach because its rhizomes are shorter and it lacks the other's ability to elongate its stem with rapid sand burial. Unlike those of marram grass, sand reed grass rhizomes also tend to dive deep for moisture rather than growing parallel with the surface. This adaptation, typical of desert plants, can be handy in times of erosion but when sand is piling up instead, sand reed grass may suffocate, its underground stem too far from the surface to get oxygen.

To tell these two commonest of foredune grasses apart in spring, look for the ring of tiny hairs on the rounded sheath, or collar, of sand reed grass where its leaf separates from the stem. Late in summer, the job is easier. Marram grass has a tall, tight-packed flowering stalk while sand reed grass bears its seeds loosely, in a wide, spreading cluster.

Little bluestem grass has some but not much of the "stretching", or elongating, ability that helps marram grass survive burial. It has no underground runners, however, nor can it make new roots from broken off stems. It can only sprout from seed. The bright blue of its joints and the brown and russet shades of its stems (fading eventually to salmon-pink) make bluestem easy to spot late in summer or in autumn. Seeds are contained in the bits of white fluff that cling to the tips of its stalks.

Hairy collar on leaves
sheathing the stem
(much enlarged)

Sand reed grass

Little bluestem

Sand cherry

Sand cherry bushes, their leaves wine-red in fall, share space with the bluestem, holding in place dunes that marram grass worked to build. These special dune shrubs have a more impoverished look, with fewer leaves and more gnarled stems than their forest cousins, pin and chokecherry shrubs. All three cherries spread by underground runners, however, and tend to cluster in thickets. The leaf of a sand cherry is narrower than the others, leathery in texture, and with few or no teeth on the part nearest the stem. The bitter fruits grow singly, one to a stalk, rather than in bunches as do those of other wild cherries. The trunks of all cherries are reddish with white dots or horizontal streaks called lenticels on their bark.

The kingbird, gray-backed and white-breasted, is also a foredune tenant. Kingbirds are easiest to spot perching for their own special view of rolling hills from the branches of a cottonwood. They are likely less interested in the distant, bright patches of goldenrod and horsemint, however, than in the robber flies searching over the sand nearby for a tasty meal of velvet ants.

Almost every animal in the fiercely competitive world of the foredunes is either hunter or hunted, or both. The velvet ants prey on digger wasps, descending the wasp burrows to lay their own eggs while the wasps vie with the kingbird to capture and dine on the robber flies.

White tiger beetle larvae, not so mobile in their infant state as adult beetles or the other dune predators, peer out from their foot-deep burrows with tiny eyes centered in the tops of their heads, ready to snatch with lightning-fast jaws any unwary insects passing overhead.

The animals, like plants of the open dunes, also have special adaptations that help them survive extremes of heat and cold.

The velvet ant has a fine, hair-like covering to insulate it, while tiger beetles and burrowing spiders live out most of their lives in burrows underground.

The white tiger beetle and the white grasshopper of the

dunes are able to forage by day without discomfort because their light color reflects heat.

Digger wasps protect themselves with special behavior patterns, like people on the beach wearing scanty swimsuits and diving into the lake on a warm day. The wasps dig their burrows fast and in short spurts, darting upward a foot or so between each thrust to where the air may be as much as ten degrees cooler than at the sand's surface. Air at the surface of foredune sand on a hot summer day may reach 135 degrees Fahrenheit.

The farther inland you walk across the grassy dunes, the greater the variety in plants and animals. Many of the old familiar species from the first ridges continue to grow and bloom and shed their seeds, but on the slopes of every new hill another plant or two crops up, a new lizard or mouse or beetle scurries for cover from your unfamiliar footfalls.

Wormwood and wild rye turn up once in a while on the open beach, but they first become common on the front dunes' lee sides and along slopes and peaks of the second and third hills. Solitary sand thistles, tiny rock cress, and clumps of prickly pear sprout here and there among them.

The lee sides of dunes, with their southern exposures and protection from lake breezes, tend to support more plants—

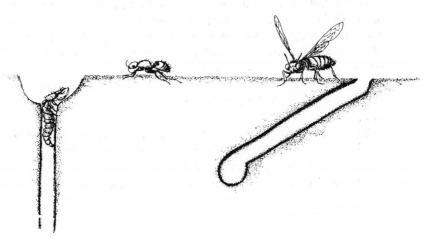

Insects of the foredunes. From left to right: tiger beetle larva in its burrow, velvet ant, digger wasp and burrow.

sometimes entirely different plants—from those on the cold north slopes. In spring these lee side plants also come up first, sometimes as much as two weeks before their neighbors on the other side of each hill.

Prickly pear is the dunes' only cactus, its round, fat pads with their sharp-pointed spikes impossible to mistake for those of any other local plant. Yellow prickly pear blossoms attract pollen-gathering insects and human photographers in great numbers in mid-summer. The plant's purplish berries can be eaten peeled and raw but taste better in jelly.

Wild rye plants grow singly or in small bunches on foredunes, their seed spikes thick and bristly, drooping above all straight stems.

Prickly pear

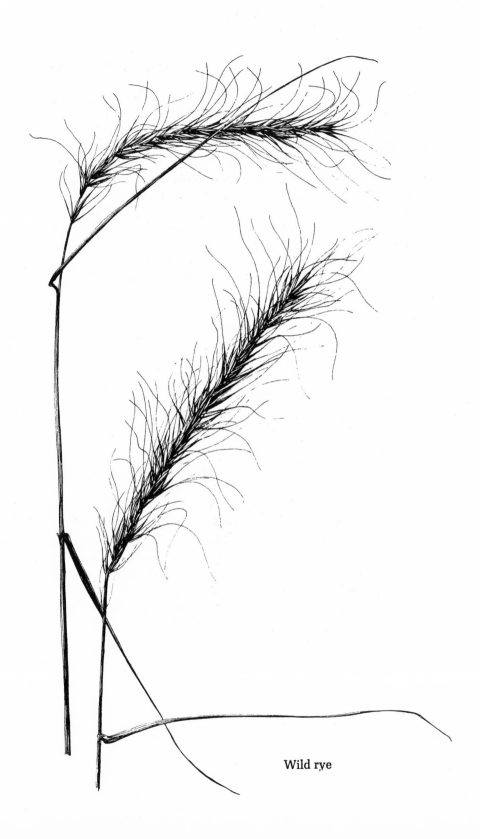

Wild rye

Wormwood, with the more appealing Latin name of Artemisia, has narrow many-forked leaves. It's a biennial, a plant that takes two years to produce seeds, and in its first year tiny white hairs overlaying the leaves' green surface give it a downy, dusty look. Tightly-closed, greenish-white specks, its flowers appear on gangly red stalks in the plant's second summer and the texture of its leaves becomes coarser.

Sand thistle, another biennial found only on Great Lakes sand dunes, is also soft-textured and fragile-looking in its youth. However, its thorn-tipped leaves, deeply lobed and narrower than those of most other thistles, reflect the harsh desert environment that nurtured it. Sand thistle flowers are cream-colored.

Sand cress, a plant that seems to turn up on every foredune and sandy black oak hillside, is easy to identify because it's about three times as tiny and delicate-looking as most of its companions. Its flowers are white with four petals, and the leaves in a circle at its base are long and curly, deeply lobed. Upper leaves, long but without lobes, are sparse.

The profusion of plants that surrounds you by the time you've reached the fourth or fifth hill in your morning's stroll makes it harder to pick out the green grasses that shaped the landscape originally.

The goldenrod of the dunes, Gillman's goldenrod, showy goldenrod, or hybrids of these and other species, become common at this point. So does hairy puccoon, a plant that starts producing flowers in April or May and keeps up the job into August.

Gillman's goldenrod in its pure form has yellow-gold blossoms on long slender stalks. The leaves at its base are long, too, and coarsely toothed.

Puccoon has yellow, five-lobed flowers and long, slender, alternate leaves with a texture that explains why it's called hairy.

Sand cress   Deer mouse   Wormwood early in summer

Sand thistle

Wormwood in late summer   Goldenrod

Hairy puccoon

Several kinds of milkweed thrive inland on foredunes. Among the most obvious are the common, pink-flowered kind and the bushier, orange-blossomed butterfly weed. The individual flowers of both plants are tiny and similar in shape. Otherwise, they look quite different.

Common milkweed has wide, velvety leaves and stout stems that exude a milky juice when broken. Its large, pointed seed pods give it a striking appearance even in winter. The narrower leaves of butterfly weed tend to droop, and its stems have no milky juice.

Horsemint has square stems and strong-smelling leaves like all the other mints but distinguishes itself by its showy, purplish-white bracts, the leaves that hold its flowers. The flowers themselves are pale yellow with red dots, in shape like the wide open jaws of some small, hungry animal.

Evening primrose grows on a tall, thick stalk with abundant, long, lance-shaped leaves. Its yellow flowers are divided into four broad petals, each one gently notched in the middle.

Short-tailed shrews, deer mice and white-footed mice are the commonest of foredune mammals, but this desert garden also includes the six-lined race runner, a yellow and brown striped lizard which would seem to be more at home in the arid lands of Arizona or New Mexico.

Seed-eating birds like field sparrows and chipping sparrows feed here in summer. Sparrows are small, brownish birds with cone-shaped bills. Both of these have rusty caps and unstreaked breasts, so you have to look closely for the chipping sparrow's white eye stripe and the field sparrow's pink bill.

Snout beetles dine on dune grasses, and the killdeer, a shorebird with brown back and two black collar stripes above its white breast, dines on snout beetles and grasshoppers.

After several generations of these plants and animals have lived and died on the dunes, their decaying remains have darkened the sand and made it porous, completely different in look and feel from the close-packed, pale sand of the beach. It can hold moisture now and support entirely new kinds of plants and animals.

Monarch butterfly caterpillar

A milkweed flower (much enlarged)

Common milkweed

butterfly weed

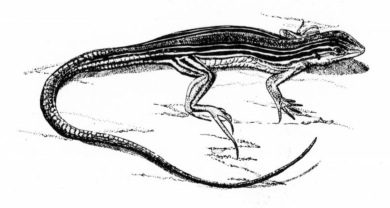

Six-lined racerunner

Horse mint   Evening primrose

A band of shrubs and vines makes an edge for most fore-dunes, separating their open, grassy expanses from the cool forests beyond. Hop trees and fragrant sumac line up in rows along this border. Poison ivy, orange-berried bittersweet, and riverbank grape wind their stems around the shrubs while pink-flowered pasture roses add their own bright patches of color and patches of starry false solomon's seal make a ground cover.

The first three have leaves that look much alike—all of them with three leaflets on the leafstalks that extend from their stems. The leaflet at the tip of the stalk on poison ivy, however, is separated from the other two leaflets by a strip of bare stalk about half an inch long. The leaflets of the hop tree and fragrant sumac grow much closer together.

Hop trees grow bigger than the other two plants, from ten to twenty-five feet tall. Their bark is smooth, light gray, shallowly grooved, and warty. Twigs are brownish and round and give off a rank odor when broken. Leaflets are usually smooth-edged, without teeth, and some of the hop trees found on Great Lakes sand dunes have leaves and twigs more velvety, better able to hold moisture, than those found elsewhere.

The tree's small flowers are greenish white and grow in clusters May to July. Its fruit, which forms in late summer and clings to the stalks through winter, is buff-colored and wafer-shaped, with a broad, veined wing. Another name for the hop tree is wafer ash.

Fragrant sumac is a rambling shrub usually no more than six feet high, though it can grow to ten feet. Its name comes from the strong aroma its leaves give off when crushed. Its twigs are brown, its bark much smoother than that of hop trees, and its flowers, which bloom in April and May, are small, greenish white, and cluster in dense spikes. In June and July there are hairy, small red berries; but the upright stalks that bear the flowers and fruits protrude, naked, from the ends of the twigs all winter.

Poison ivy, a close relative of the fragrant sumac, is the member of this particular trio which gave rise to the saying, "Leaves of three; let it be." All of its parts—leaves, stem, root, flowers, and berries—contain a dangerous skin irritant

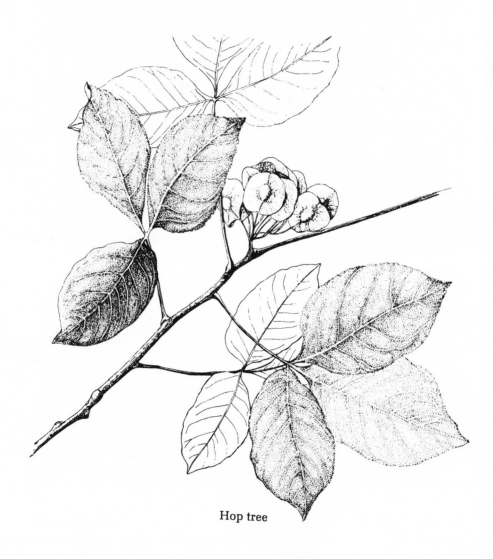

Hop tree

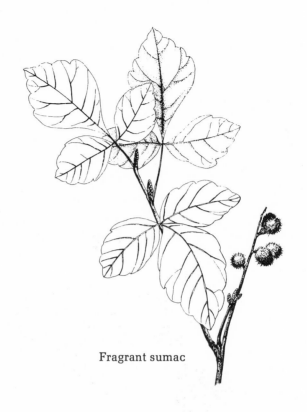

Fragrant sumac

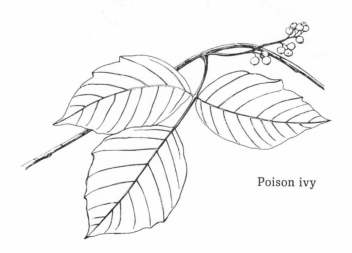

Poison ivy

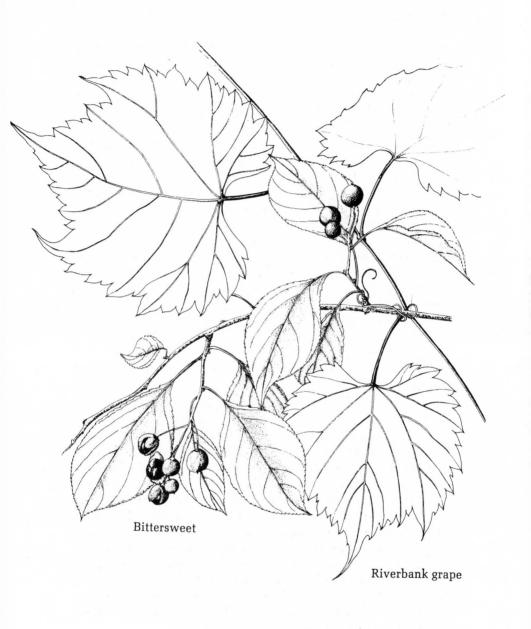

Bittersweet

Riverbank grape

which can be transmitted to people who either touch a plant or inhale fumes when it's burning. The leaves of poison ivy are always three-parted, but otherwise one plant of the species may look much different from another. It can grow as an upright shrub, a trailing vine, or it may snake its way up a tree with the aid of special aerial roots. The leaves may be stiff and leathery, glossy or dull, hairy beneath or smooth, coarse-toothed, and wavy-edged—or neither. Very young and dying leaves are reddish; others are green.

The old stems of climbing poison ivy vines have dark, stringy fibers and may completely cover the bark of a host tree. Its buds are plainly visible in summer, unlike those of hop trees and fragrant sumac shrubs. The flowers of poison ivy are small and greenish-white, blooming in clusters from May to July. The berries are white and may linger from August to midwinter. Virginia creeper, another climbing vine, looks like poison ivy at a distance, but its leaflets grow in groups of five rather than three.

Bittersweet and riverbank grape are also vines that twine about the shrubs and young trees at the edge of the foredunes. Bittersweet has egg-shaped, pointy-tipped, wavy-toothed leaves that fold in half lengthwise down their midribs in summer's heat. Its flowers are greenish, clustered, and not very conspicuous; but its fruits are bright orange pods that fold back late in summer to reveal even brighter scarlet seed coverings. These berries usually cling to the plant past Christmas.

Grapes are already familiar to most people, because the wild species look so much like those that grow in backyard gardens. They have broad, heart-shaped leaves, usually toothed, and thornless, shreddy-barked stems. Riverbank grape, the type most common to foredunes, can be told from its sometime companion, the summer grape, by its leaves, which have more pointed teeth on the margins and are green (and sometimes woolly) underneath. Summer grape leaves are either reddish-brown or white and always woolly underneath. Grapes flower in May and June and bear their tasty blue-black fruits in August and September.

Pasture rose

Starry false solomon's seal

Starry false solomon's seal is an herbaceous plant, eight to twenty inches tall, with oval, pointed leaves that alternate, clasping, on a long stem. Its tiny white flowers cluster at the stem's tip. Its berries are greenish with black stripes, turning to solid black late in summer.

The wild roses of foredune edges are the same pink-flowered pasture roses that soften the edges of abandoned barns in old fields and line the ditches of country roadsides. They are distinguished from other roses by their straight thorns that grow opposite each other on their stems. A paler rose, nearly thornless, called smooth or early wild rose, may also be found in the band of shrubs between foredune and woods.

WANDERING DUNES, BLOWOUTS, AND INTERDUNAL PONDS

The plants that build dunes don't always win their battles against the wind. A marram grass dune may be worn away entirely in a winter of fierce storms and heavy ice, leaving steep, wave-cut cliffs where gentle slopes met the beach the previous autumn. Kingfishers and bank swallows love the cliffs, for they lend themselves well to nesting holes. But little bluestem and sand reed grasses, used to having a buffer hill between their territory and the wind-charged lake, languish with the unaccustomed exposure.

If lake levels are high and storms are bad for several years in a row, foredunes with their bright flower and grass cover may disappear entirely, leaving pines or black oak forests leaning from the cliffs above the beach.

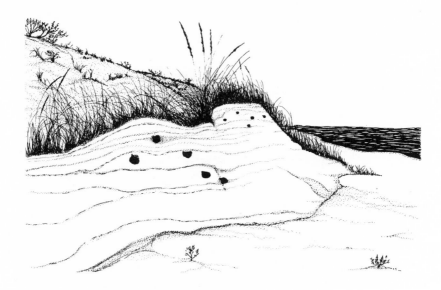

Bank swallow nesting holes in an eroded foredune

The wind doesn't always erase the handiwork of past seasons so completely, however. Sometimes it merely carves a narrow channel through the tangle of plant roots holding a dune together, seeking for its excavation route a ribbon of sand worn bare by hikers' feet or a low spot in a ridge where two separate dunes have grown together. The narrow channel may eventually deepen and widen until a huge amphitheater is formed: in dunes terminology it's called a "blowout," sometimes a quarter of a mile long and five or six hundred yards wide.

Wandering dunes, huge bare hills of sand that move inland *en masse*, burying forests, swamps, and summer cottages in their wake with steamroller-like impartiality, are also agents of the wind. They start when sand piles up too rapidly for even the fast-growing rhizomes of marram grass to spread their nets wide or dive deep enough to reach stored moisture. A solitary dune-former like the cottonwood may also free a dune to move at the whims of the wind when the tree dies of old age or accident and falls over.

If blowouts and wandering dunes didn't exist, the landscape of dune country would be monotonously regular, row after row of neat, low, parallel sand ridges facing the lake. Because of them, we have instead mounds of every shape and size, extending in every direction behind the shores of our own familiar Lake Michigan and the beaches of prehistoric Lake Chicago farther inland. The unusually high dunes, in particular, are the products of wind erosion. Mount Tom in Indiana Dunes State Park, towering 192 feet above the lake, is a blowout ridge. Mount Baldy in the National Lakeshore is an active dune 123 feet tall that still wanders south some four feet a year. Both were formed when moving dunes climbed over the tops of previously existing ridges.

Trees like oak and hickory that occupy the middle ground between dry desert and wet swamp die quickly when moving dunes sweep over them. The leaves of black oaks on the lee side of Mount Baldy dry and turn brown in midsummer when sand has piled less than a quarter of the way up their trunks.

Swamp forests when overtaken last much longer. The characteristics that helped their species survive flooding in damper habitats also keep them from smothering in sand.

The windward slopes of moving dunes are usually bare of vegetation other than small scattered wisps of beach annuals like bugseed and occasional clumps of marram grass. A curved dark line of humus about halfway up their slopes may be the first visible sign of a forest buried deep beneath the surface.

The dry sand does not promote decay, so when the dune has passed on, the dead trees are often still standing, their original forms intact but their color changed from bright greens and browns to a ghostly gray-black. Some may be several hundred years old. At Indiana Dunes, these forests are called tree graveyards.

Dunes in Indiana have been known to move as fast as sixty feet a year, but their speed slows gradually with distance from the lake or when a new foredune or other obstacle is formed to windward. To learn whether a once-moving dune has stopped, one can peer down its leeward side to see if plants are beginning to creep up the slope. Marram grass and grapevines are often the first to take hold. Common milkweed, starry false solomon's seal, and sand reed grass appear soon after.

The starry false solomon's seal is one of two species of false solomon's seal found frequently at the dunes. Both have oval, pointed leaves that alternate on a long stem, and both have clusters of tiny white flowers at the stem's tip. (True solomon's seals have flowers at leaf axils all along the stem).

The starry species of false solomon's seal seems better able to survive sand burial and to thrive on freshly eroded dune surfaces. Common false solomon's seal becomes "common" in the sense of occurring in great numbers only on stable ground in deep woods.

In places where the two grow together, you can tell them apart in late summer by the berries. Those of starry false solomon's seal are greenish with black stripes, turning to solid black. The berries of common false solomon's seal are whitish speckled with brown, then ruby red. The stalk of the common species tends to droop while the starry has a more erect posture. The leaves of common false solomon's seal are between one and three inches wide, those of the starry twice as narrow (one-half to one-and-a-half inches).

The bowls of blowouts, like the windward slopes of wandering dunes, have little vegetation in their earliest stages. Plants eventually begin to creep down from the ridges that surround them, however. It may happen when the amphitheaters have grown so wide and long that the effects of wind are dissipated or when the surface has been scoured down level with the beach and a new foredune grows, blocking the wind's entrance from the lake side.

Seeds blown in or carried by birds may also lodge and sprout in the damp depressions of a blowout's center. Most of the stabilized blowouts at Indiana Dunes have a row of cottonwoods down the middle of these depressions. Sand cherry, willow, and red osier dogwood shrubs tend to sprout there, too, along with straight, sectioned stalks of scouring rush, the kind that looks like miniature bamboo fishing poles.

The cottonwood and sand cherry are the same species found on the foredunes. Willows and red osier dogwood grow sometimes on foredunes, too, but they thrive in greater numbers in low protected swales.

Willows seem to interbreed with abandon, so that it's often

difficult to tell one species from another. All of them have alternate leaves, though, usually longer than wide, and in spring they bear flowers in long furry catkins, the sexes on separate plants. They have round, limber stems that make them ideal for basket weaving, and their leaves turn yellow in fall. They tend to cluster in thickets, and they can be separated from similar shrubs in winter by the single scale on their buds.

The willows that thrive in dune country, like all the other plants there, show the effects of their harsh, dry home. Some, like the sandbar willows, fight evaporation with long, narrow leaves that expose as little surface as possible to the sun's rays. Others, like the furry dune willow special to Great Lakes sand dunes, have wider leaves and hold moisture with a thick, downy covering on both their leaves and stems. Blue-leaved willow, another dunes native, has a leathery leaf that not only reflects light and heat but resists the wind's sand-blasting with its tough surface.

Red osier dogwood can be distinguished from other dog-woods by its bright red, almost purple, stem. Its small white flowers grow in clusters, unlike those of its cousin, the showy flowering dogwood of deep woods, which has large, single, petal-like bracts—white with pinkish-red notches at their tips.

The berries of red osier dogwood in summer are white, too. It shares its gently curving leaf veins with others of its genus, and its leaves grow in matched pairs, opposite each other on their stems. (The only native dogwood with leaves not in matched pairs has been appropriately dubbed the alternate-leaved dogwood).

The scouring rush of blowout centers is a relative of the familiar horsetail found in damp roadside ditches. It lacks the long broomstraw branches, though, and so looks more like miniature cane. Its stems come apart in neat sections at their black-fringed joints, like a backpacker's fishing rod. At the tip of the plant's bright green stem is a dome-shaped (or some-

Dune willow

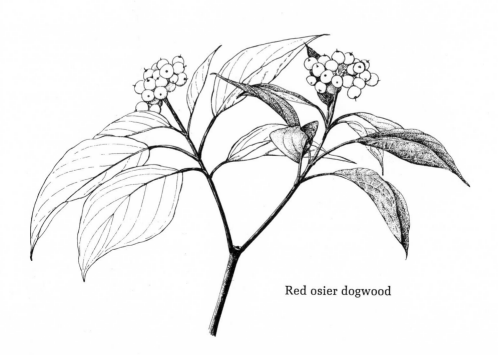

Red osier dogwood

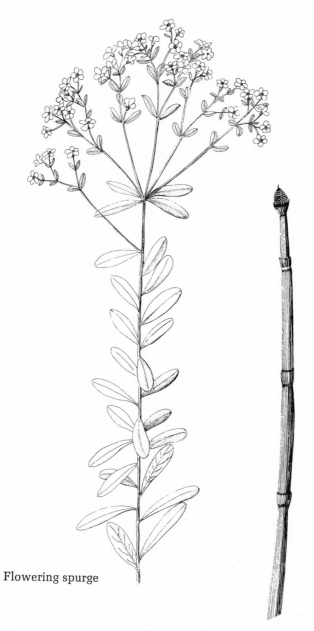

Flowering spurge

Tall scouring rush

times pointed) black or black-and-white-striped cap.

Most of a blowout's flat surface is covered by the same plants one sees on foredunes. The familiar grasses are there—marram, sand reed, wild rye, and little bluestem—and many of the flowers—wormwood and puccoon, common milkweed and sand thistle, horsemint, and goldenrod.

A plant called flowering spurge, relative of the seaside spurge found on dune beaches, sometimes thrives on blowout slopes, though it becomes much more common inland along the sunny edges of woodland trails and in prairie openings of oak forests. Its small white flowers rise from five or six thin stems above a whorl of long, green leaves. The leaves on the plant's main stem below the whorl are alternate. Flowering spurge can also be told by the milky juice that exudes from the stem when it's broken.

Because the floor of a blowout is flat, organic matter from decaying plants and animals builds quicker there than on exposed and sloping foredunes, and the acorns of black and white oaks dropped by chipmunks and squirrels may produce thriving young trees.

Hop trees grow in blowouts as they do on the wooded edge of foredunes, and pines and junipers edge down from the tops of the ridges. Junipers found at the dunes come in two types, the tall, thin-spired red cedar species and the short, square clumps of common, or dwarf, juniper. White pines, with their long elegant needles, stay mostly on the tops of blowout ridges. Jack pines hang from the slopes and even grow sometimes on flat blowout bottoms.

The animals that thrive in blowouts tend to be the same ones that flourish on foredunes unless the wind has scoured sand so deep in the bowl that it reaches water level. When that happens, interdunal ponds are formed. There are five big ones strung out in a row between the sand hills of West Beach. In dry weather, their shorelines shrink and they separate into ten or twelve smaller ponds. Some sources call these bodies of water intradunal ponds since they occur within a dune complex. We prefer interdunal, since they occur between dunes.

The small black insects called water treaders, water strid-

Baltic rush

Damselfly

Kalm's St. John's wort

Bog arrow grass

ers and water boatmen swim on them, while whirligig beetles dart about just above their surface and damselflies and dragonflies circle overhead, devouring mosquitoes. Young Fowlers toads seem literally to blanket the ground after spring or early summer rains.

The plants around interdunal ponds are different, too. Almost all of them have special adaptations that suit them to life in and around water, but many also have the narrow leaves, fuzzy or leathery or glossy surfaces of desert plants. The air above interdunal ponds is much blown and dried by wind, and there are no spreading shade trees nearby to shield the plants from sun.

Bulrushes and other sedges grow in the shallows along with common cattail and bog arrow grass. Bog arrow grass can be spotted most easily by the tiny, round, tufted green flowers and later by the brown, oblong fruits growing in alternate pairs along the length of its long, thick stalk. Most sedges (bulrushes are exceptions) can be told from grasses by their triangular stems. Grass stems are round. Cattails have stiff, round stems with flat, sturdy blades, but they are familiar to most people for their sausagelike, brown flowering spikes.

Baltic rush plants grow in neat rows on the pond edges, each shoot springing up from a stout, creeping rootstock called a stolon. Cottonwood shoots sprout among them, their stems still red in infancy, while willow, sand cherry, and red osier dogwood thickets gather nearby.

Killdeer

A row of Baltic rush plants showing underground stolon.

The height of flower bloom around the ponds is in late summer. Among the array is the special dune species of St. John's wort, called Kalm's St. John's wort. It has many branches with woody, two-edged twigs and is crowned with masses of five-petaled, golden flowers. Its leaves are long, smooth-edged, and narrower than those of a similar species, shrubby St. Johns wort.

The upland white, or stiff, aster also blooms in July, its small flower rays grouped in a flat-topped cluster with yellow discs in their centers that turn a purplish-brown before summer is over. The leaves of this aster are thin and grasslike, toothless and glossy-looking, poking out stiffly without leafstalks, from the plant's central stem.

Purple gerardias and rose pinks blend their bright shades in August with the pale blue petals of Kalm's lobelia. The rare yellow horned bladderwort mingles sparsely among them.

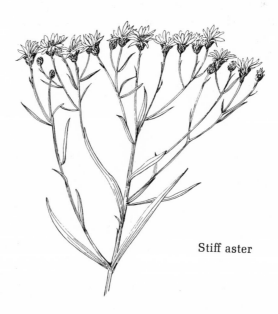

Stiff aster

Rose pink

Purple gerardia

Short-fruited rush

Kalm's lobelia

Young Fowler's toads

Horned bladderwort

The blossoms of rose pink, five-petaled with yellow centers, grow from stalks that branch in pairs from square stems. The plant's broad, toothless leaves come in pairs. They hug their stem tightly, without a connecting leafstalk (the botanical term for such leaves is "sessile.").

Gerardia, a member of the snapdragon family, has deep, bell-shaped flowers that grow from its leaf axils. (An axil is the angle between a central stem and the leaf that grows from it). The leaves themselves are thin and grasslike.

Kalm's lobelia is smaller and paler in color than most other lobelias. It has a tiny white eye in its center and its leaves are grasslike, growing alternately, as do the flowers, from its stem. The lobelias around the interdunal ponds space themselves in tussocks.

Horned bladderwort grows at water's edge or in mud on the pond margins and has yellow blossoms with long, drooping spurs. Its "bladders," tiny hollow sacs that project from its narrow underwater or underground leaves, capture swimming insects like water fleas and mosquito larvae which the plant then digests for the nitrogen they provide.

In autumn, fringed gentian and nodding ladies' tresses bloom among the grasses.

The fringed gentian was named for the swirl of four delicately-fringed petals that flare out from the deep bell of its purple blossoms. Each corolla of the flower, nestled in a cupped green sheath called a calyx, grows from a single long stalk. Leaves are pointed and grow in pairs.

Nodding ladies tresses, a kind of orchid, has delicate white flowers that grow in a double spiral on a long, slender stem. The plant's leaves, slender also, cluster at its base.

EVERGREEN TREES AND
BEARBERRIES

Great groves of white pines once blanketed the sandy hills of Lake Michigan's southern shore. They were cut down in the 1830s and 1840s, transformed into tidy stacks of flat, sturdy boards, and shipped off to build the city of Chicago. Remnants of these huge forests tower in solitary splendor from the tallest hills on inland dunes today and mingle in sparse stands among oak and maple woodlands. They have long graceful needles, clustered in bundles of five, and slender, tapering cones. Their bark is darker and less scaly than that of other pines, tending rather to shape itself in deep furrows.

The evergreens most important to current dunes ecology, however, are the less noble-looking but still indomitable jack pines, red cedars, and clumps of common juniper. They are the first trees after cottonwoods to get a start on windward slopes and the crests of dunes near the lake, and they often string out in a long, narrow band to make a buffer with shrubs like sumac and red osier dogwood between windblown foredunes and deciduous oak forests.

Jack pines also cluster in low, chilly pockets between dunes, either on the floors of old blowouts sealed off from the lake by several rows of foredunes or at the edge of sedge swamps among the ancient dunes that graced the shores of Lake Chicago in prehistoric times.

The jack pines are so well adapted to cold and other harsh conditions that their range extends farther north into the taiga of Canada than any other pine. The outer skin of their needle-like leaves is so thick that it forms half the bulk of the entire needle, and their stomata openings, the pores through which a leaf "breathes," are sunk deep into each needle's lower surface. Jack pines can grow in humus-free dune sand as well as in the sterile frozen ground of the Far North, because they need only small quantities of the soil nutrients, like calcium, that hardwood trees require. Jack pine needles are much shorter than those of white pines and grow in bundles of two. Their cones are between an inch and two inches long and usually curve at the tip. The trees' gray to reddish brown bark has a scaly, rough appearance.

They form, at Indiana Dunes, an isolated colony, more than sixty miles south of any other jack pine grove around the Great Lakes. Their existence there is another reminder that a glacier once passed this way. When climates began to warm again at the end of the last Ice Age, most northern plants retreated gradually along with the ice. The islands of boreal forest vegetation that remain, in places like the tops of the Great Smoky Mountains in Tennessee and at Indiana Dunes, do so only in patches where more widely adaptive, temperate zone plants can't grow.

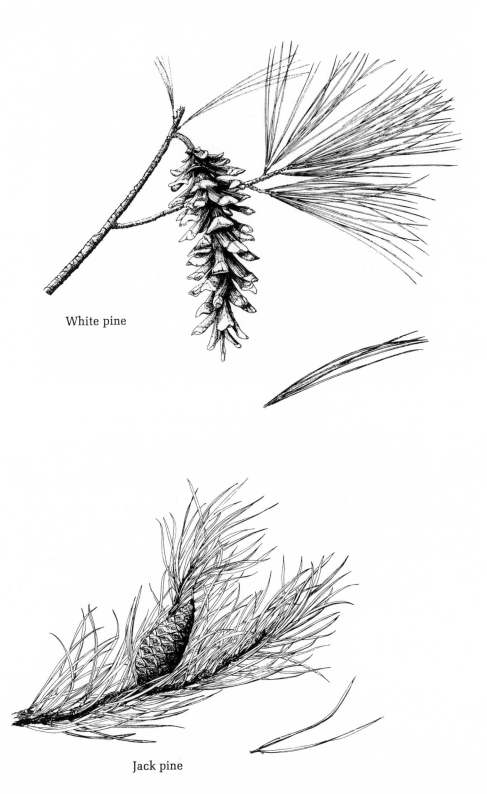

White pine

Jack pine

The bearberry, a low, woody creeper of the heath family, is another of these Northern Forest plants. It occurs in many different habitats at the dunes, but has a very special relationship with the jack pine in particular. Bearberries, like marram grass, starry false solomon's seal, and many other dune plants, spread by sending up new shoots from underground runners. They usually take hold only on dunes already stabilized by some other pioneer, however, because, while bearberries can survive slow sand burial, they don't grow fast enough to stay ahead of really rapid pile-up.

This is the same sort of environment that suits the jack pine. But since jack pines don't have rhizomes and each one must start from seed, the bearberry provides a ground cover just dense enough to protect the young pines from wind and blowing sand until they're big enough and strong enough to fend for themselves.

The bearberry has papery, reddish stems and small, paddle-shaped, evergreen leaves that grow from the base to the tip of each stem. Its flowers are bell-shaped, white with delicate pink tips, and its berries in late summer are bright red.

Bearberry

The dunes' two species of juniper, the squat common kind and the tall, skinny red cedar, also appear often on dune slopes or blowouts before the taller jack and white pines. Junipers look different from pines because their needles grow singly rather than in bundles from their twigs; and their fruits, round and blue-gray, coated with a white powder, look more like berries than the typical cones of most evergreens. Red cedars have scalelike leaves as well as distinctive, three-sided needles, the two types often appearing on the same tree.

The common, or dwarf, juniper of the dunes has needles that grow around the stems in whorls of three, and the upper surface of its needles has a white streak running down the center.

The kinds of animals and understory plants found among the pines and junipers reflect the kinds of habitats that surround the evergreens as much as any special climate created by the evergreens themselves.

Pine groves near the lake provide homes for foredune animals like burrowing and crab spiders, black ants and six-lined racerunner lizards, blue racers and garter snakes. The tiger beetle of the pines is the bronze species, and pitch moths feed on the resin of new pine shoots.

Birds partial to dune pines include long-eared and great-horned owls that seek the cover of evergreen foliage in winter and four kinds of finches (evening grosbeaks, pine siskins, red crossbills, and white-winged crossbills) that gather in great numbers some winters at the dunes but are virtually absent in others.

The plants that grow around and beneath the scattered jack pines on windward dune slopes and wave-cut cliffs above the beach are mainly the grasses and foredune flowers that were there before the trees.

On the floors of old blowouts the pines share space with willows and red osier dogwoods, while on blowout slopes and the tops of blowout ridges, grapes and bittersweet twine among their needles. White pines can also be found on the tops of such ridges.

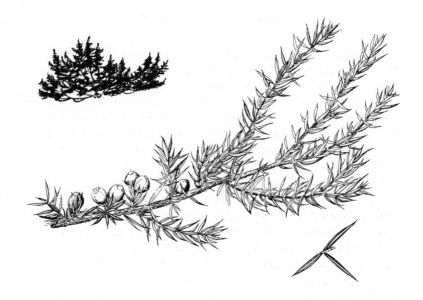

Common juniper

Red cedar

On the edges of foredunes, poison ivy and starry false solomon's seal take advantage of the pine's shade, helping to build layers of rich humus that will eventually enable oaks and hickories to displace the evergreens.

Aromatic sumac bushes and young hop trees, bittersweet, and grapevines share this border territory, too, along with pink-flowered pasture rose with its straight thorns and the near-thornless, paler pink, smooth rose.

In deeper woods and on slopes above the edges of swamps, the flowers that grow beneath pines are the same ones that grow in the surrounding hardwood forests: may apples and Canada mayflowers, wintergreen with its spicy-tasting leaves, bellwort, wild strawberry, early meadow rue, and sweet cicely.

HARDWOOD DUNES AND COVES

The gentle ridges where oaks grow at Indiana Dunes were thousands of years in the making. Time has been ample for drought and fires and flood, hot and cold climates, changes in the very shape of the land to build a thousand different communities of plants and animals. They thrive still, the variety evident in a walk along any dune trail. Every hilltop and hollow, open meadow, and deeply-shaded glen has its own special character, its own small but self-contained ecosystem.

Black oak trees dominate nearly all the ridges, but there the similarity ends. The youngest tree-covered dunes, those that

77

were bare sand shore some time in the last eight thousand
years of shrinking Great Lakes shorelines, are scrubby and
open, savannas by and large, with prairie grasses and sedge
meadows, choke cherry and witch hazel.

Blueberry thickets begin to appear on dunes of Lake Chicago's Tolleston beach period, hills that are between eight
and ten thousand years old. Frequent fires, natural and man-
made, over centuries have kept the landscape open, especially
on dry ridge tops and windward slopes.

Low, moist pockets of woodland, even those very near the
lake, have a richer growth, more different kinds of trees, more
varied vines and wildflowers, fewer shrubs.

The oldest dunes of all, those dating from the Calumet and
Glenwood stages of Lake Michigan's broader-shored ancestor,
have been affected less by fire, partly because the ridges are
farther and more protected from lake wind influences, closer
to the meandering bed of the Little Calumet River.

There are black oaks still on these older dunes, mixed now
and again with red oaks and sugar maples. Blueberries aren't
as abundant on the very oldest Glenwood dunes, but groves
of black cherries and red raspberry bushes make up for the
loss in trail snacks, and carpets of trillium and hepatica in
spring are thicker there than in any other section of dune
forest.

Dr. Cowles wondered, when he studied sand dunes at the
turn of the century, if someday great beech forests would take
over the oldest dune ridges here at the southern end of the lake
as they had already done in his day on the Sleeping Bear
dunes of Michigan and in flatland forests of Indiana south of
the Kankakee River. They haven't done so yet, and modern
dune researchers, scientists like the late Dr. Charles Olmsted
and Dr. Jerry Olson, while they were at Cowles' own University of Chicago, have speculated they never will.

There are beech trees at the dunes but they are few and far
between, isolated interlopers in scattered damp hollows, behind Chellberg Farm, for instance, in the National Lakeshore,

or in the lowland forest that borders Dune Creek in the State Park. Once black oaks take hold, it seems, they allow nutrients not needed for their growth to leach away and leave a soil that's too poor ever to nourish the likes of trees like beech that need piles of mineral-rich humus.

The climate at Sleeping Bear in Michigan is damper, too, and the sand dunes there, climbing over rock and clay, are higher and steeper. The evergreen trees of Michigan dunes are also different, red pines and hemlocks instead of the jack pines that grow on the lake's south shore.

So Indiana dune country, with all the variety it contains, has turned out also to be different from dunes everywhere else, even those nearby on other Great Lakes shores.

Oak Savannas

One kind of oak often looks much like another, and amateur naturalists may tend to give up in despair. The two commonest that grow on Lake Michigan and Tolleston dunes, however (all State Park and National Lakeshore land north of U.S. 12) are, luckily for observers, very dissimilar.

The ubiquitous black oak of the dunes belongs to a group of trees called the red or black oak group which have leaves with sharp-pointed lobes and bitter, inedible acorns.

The white oak common to the area lends its name to the white oak group, trees that have round-lobed leaves, pale bark, and sweet-tasting acorns.

The profiles of black and white oaks in winter are different, too. Black oak branches angle sharply upward while white oak branches stick straight out from their trunks.

The shrubs that thrive with the oaks on the youngest dunes are choke cherry, witch hazel, and shadbush, winged and fragrant sumac. When you see a blueberry thicket, you'll know you're walking on a dune that's at least eight thousand years old.

Choke cherry has the same rich, reddish-brown, white-dotted bark as other cherries, but its finely-toothed leaves are

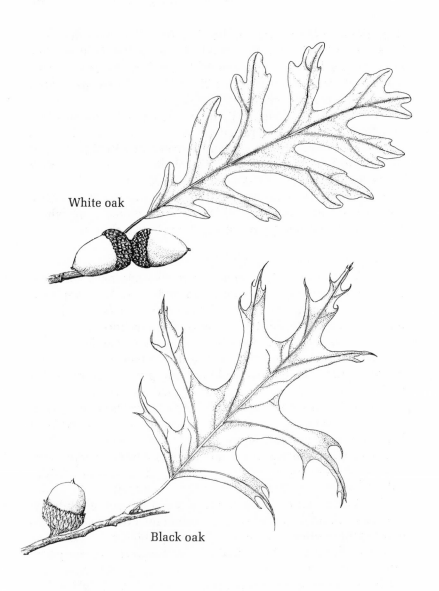

White oak

Black oak

much broader than those of other dune cherries, and its white flowers and bitter. fruits (the choke cherry is well-named) grow strung out on long "racemes," or stalks. Sand cherry fruits grow singly, and those of pin cherry are bunched. Black cherries grow in racemes, but black cherry trees old enough to produce fruit are already much taller than their shrubby cousins.

Witch hazel, so named because country folk used to believe its branches, used as divining rods, could lead them to water, is probably the commonest and most widespread of all shrubs in dune country. It is most distinctive in fall, because its threadlike yellow flowers bloom after other plants have begun to lose their leaves and go into winter dormancy. The flowers come after the previous year's seed pods have burst open, shooting the seeds, slingshot-like, sometimes as far as twenty feet. Another name for witch hazel is snapping hazel. The opened pods cling to the plant all winter, making identification easy. The leaves of witch hazel are oval-shaped, coarse-surfaced with wavy edges and uneven bases.

Shadbush, in contrast to the witch hazel, is most easily identified in early spring, when its drooping, five-petaled white flowers offer almost the only visual relief from still bare and brown winter woods. On the east coast, shadbush blooms at the same time shad migrate up tidal rivers to spawn. Thus the tree came by one of its names. (It is also called juneberry and serviceberry.) Shadbush buds are different from those of other shrubs—pink to reddish, slender, with dark-tipped twisted scales. Leaves are oval or elliptical, toothed, with long, pointed tips, and the berries, red at first, dark blue when ripe, are said to be good in jellies. Two species of shadbush are common at the dunes. They look almost identical to an amateur's eyes.

The fragrant sumac that intrudes on oak forests is the same shrub that made a border for foredunes, different from other sumacs in having but three leaflets on each leaf stalk.

Winged sumac is more typical of its genus, having any-

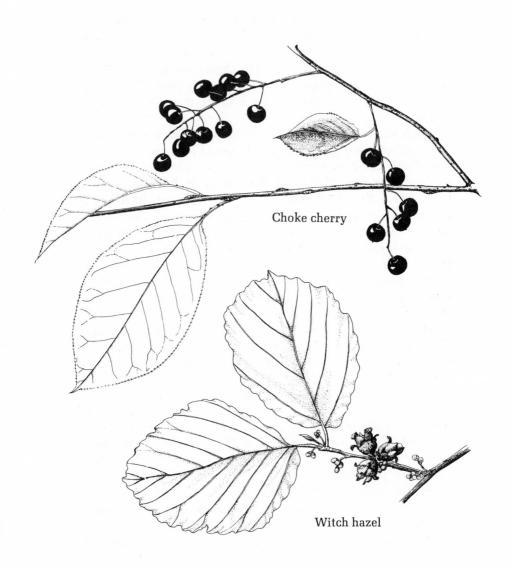

Choke cherry

Witch hazel

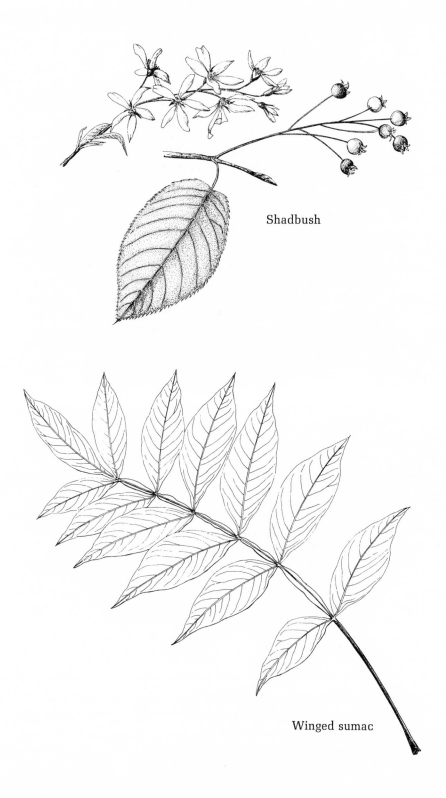

Shadbush

Winged sumac

where from a dozen to two dozen leaflets in opposing pairs except for the end one on each stalk. Its flowers and fruits are also like those of most other sumacs, the flowers small and greenish-white, the fruits red and hairy, growing in dense spikes. The characteristic that makes winged sumac special is the leafy wing or border running along each side of its leafstalk. It has pale, raised dots on its bark.

There are two kinds of lowbush blueberries on open, sandy dune savannas, an early fruiting variety and a late one. Both have small, egg-shaped, short-stalked leaves and green or reddish twigs, covered with tiny speckles or warts. Their flowers are bell-shaped and white, edged delicately with pink.

The early-berried bush grows bigger, up to three feet, and has larger leaves, as much as two inches long and one-and-a-half inches wide. Late lowbush blueberry grows to two feet and its leaves are narrower, seldom more than half an inch wide.

Late low blueberry

Early low blueberry

Black huckleberry bushes grow on the open oak dunes, too, about the same height as early blueberry bushes but with leaves even bigger, one to three inches long and covered on both sides with yellow resin-dots. Huckleberry blossoms are clustered, greenish white or greenish red. Blueberry fruits have a white, powdery coating which huckleberries lack. To tell which is which for sure, try biting into one and counting the seeds. Huckleberries have only ten; blueberries have many more.

Many of the flowers on the black oak savannas are old familiars from the foredunes—flowering spurge, starry false solomon's seal, sand cress and hairy puccoon, prickly pear, pasture rose, wormwood, horsemint, butterfly weed, and common milkweed.

There are still little bluestem and sand reed grasses, but others begin to mix in, too, on the stable, tree-covered dunes. The commonest are june grass and several kinds of "panic grass." (The name of the latter comes from its Latin name, *Panicum,* and not from any emotional response it arouses in the eyes of observers.) Pennsylvania sedge is commonest of all, even more abundant than the black oaks themselves.

Junegrass grows a flowering stalk about a foot tall in early summer, dense but not as tightly packed as that of marram grass, and it has short, very narrow, flat leaf blades.

The panic grass commonest on black oak dunes is one called switch grass. It towers over most of its companions, growing sometimes to six feet. The flowering stalk of switch grass is loose like sand reed grass, but the collar on its leaf sheath is smooth instead of hairy.

Pennsylvania sedge has a sharp-edged stem, about eight inches high, and a thick, flowering stalk. It's the only sedge at the dunes which is conspicuous as early as April and May. You can recognize it most easily by its showy tufts of yellow anthers. (Anthers are the enlarged part of the stamen, or male flowering organ, which holds the pollen.)

The omnipresent fern of black oak dunes is the bracken

June grass   Pennsylvania sedge

fern. It appears early in spring and keeps producing new leaves all summer. Bracken is a strong, dark-green and coarse-looking fern with branching leaves.

Flowers seem to cover every patch of sunny ground mid-summers on the black oak savannas. There are too many of them to describe, except in a special field guide for wild-flowers.

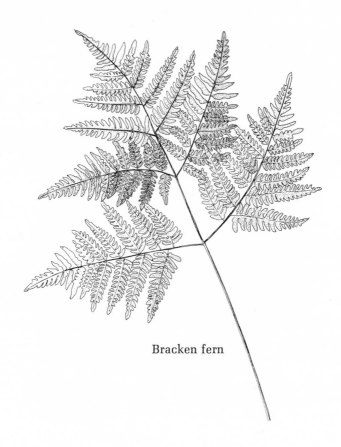

Bracken fern

Lupine

Among the showiest and best known is lupine, a member of the pea family, with blue-violet blossoms in May that look like those of domestic sweet pea. The flowers grow on short flower stalks all along a single stem between one and two feet tall. The plant's leaves are flat and palmlike, radiating into seven to nine leaflets. Lupine seed pods look like those of garden peas except they're tougher, brown, and fuzzy.

Purple-flowered birdsfoot violet thrives in sun better than other violets. It is a flower that prospered on Midwest prairies before farmers came to plow them and industrialists came to turn their flat expanses into cities like Chicago. It has five petals like others of its species, grows four to ten inches tall, and has narrow, many-forked leaves from which it got its name.

Birdsfoot violet

Other prairie plants that survive in sunny meadows of the black oak savannas at Indiana Dunes are round-headed bush clover, sky blue aster, flax-leaved aster, and various species of blazing star.

Round-headed bush clover has leaflets narrower than those of most clovers, smooth-edged, growing in groups of three from a single stalk between two and five feet tall. Its creamy white flowers, sometimes tinged with pink, grow in thick clusters at the stalk's tip.

Sky blue aster, between one and four feet tall, has bright blue or purple blossoms and smooth-edged spear-shaped leaves that widen out gradually from their leafstalks. Its lower leaves are heart-shaped.

Flax-leaved aster usually grows eight to ten inches tall, with pale blue-violet flower rays and stiff, needlelike leaves.

Blazing star rises from single, narrow-leaved stems, its purple, stringy flowers spilling over the top of scaly, modified leaves called bracts on short stalks the length of the stem. The shape of the flower bracts is the easiest way to tell one species from another. Rough blazing star, for instance, has rounded scales on its bracts. Those of cylindric blazing star have pointed tips.

Other sun lovers usually found nearby include black-eyed susans and thimbleweed, showy goldenrod, goats' rue and fern-leaved false foxglove, New Jersey tea with its odd-looking triangular fruits, and bastard toadflax, so-called because it grows as a parasite on the roots of other plants.

Ohio spiderwort, with three-petaled bright blue flowers on sturdy stalks sometimes three feet high, grows along trail edges in the black oak woods. So does yellow woodland sunflower, often single-blossomed, much smaller and more delicate than the coarse sunflowers of old farm fields, and various species of phlox. A particular phlox called sand or cleft phlox, native to the dunes, has five white or pale violet petals, deeply notched.

In small scattered patches far from roads, there is also still

Rough blazing
star

Flax-leaved aster   Round-headed bush clover   Sky-blue aster

real virgin prairie at the dunes. These patches aren't open to public access because their isolated ecosystem is too fragile to withstand the onslaught of crowds. Sometimes it's enough just to know something special is there, plants that almost justify the dunes' national park status all by themselves.

Blue hearts, among the rarest of all wildflowers in our area, grow in these prairies. So do slender ladies' tresses, Indian paintbrush and Indian plantain, rattlesnake master and false indigo, porcupine grass and big bluestem prairie grass, also known as turkey foot for the shape of the flowering stalk on its six-foot-long stem.

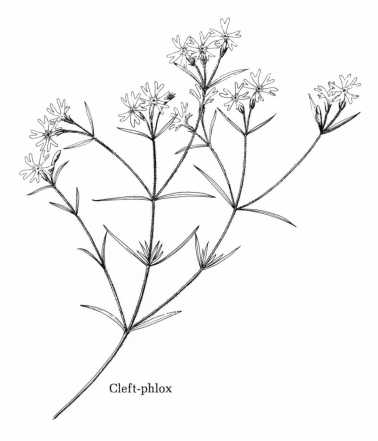

Cleft-phlox

Deep Shade

The sun-loving plants of prairies and black oak savannas disappear from the deep woods of older dunes, in parts of the state park where deliberate human management has kept fires out for more than half a century, and in low, moist hardwood coves protected from wind behind the highest of foredunes near the lake. The trees in these forests are not only bigger and older than those on the savannas, they are also more varied in kind. And the wildflowers that thrive best beneath them are those that bloom in spring and early summer, before leaves cover the trees and blot out their sunshine. Shrubs with more tolerance for shade also appear there among the witch hazels, choke cherries and blueberries of the black oak dunes. Black oaks still thrive in the deeper shade, and white oaks continue to be scattered among them. If you peer up through the canopy, though, or scuff through the leaves at your feet in fall, you will begin to notice some different leaf shapes.

Red oaks are there, shagbark and bitternut hickory, white ash and sugar maple. Basswoods dominate the lee slopes of rich forest pockets near the lake and are scattered here and there among deeply-shaded forests all over the dunes. Red oaks give their name to the group of oaks with sharp-pointed leaves. Black oaks belong to the same group. Many a beginner in field identification has been tempted to give up his hobby entirely over the frustration of trying to tell red and black oaks apart. Here are a few suggestions culled from various texts.

The widest part of a red oak leaf is supposed to be midway between base and tip. Black oaks are widest near the tip. The acorns of red oaks in fall have shallower cups. Buds and new twigs of the two trees show the most striking difference, however. Black oak buds are pale and woolly and sharply angled. Those of red oaks are reddish brown and not angled at all. The twigs of both are reddish brown, but those of red oak are supposed to be smooth while those of black oak have conspicuous lenticels, small dots or streaks like those on cherry trees.

The hickories have alternate compound leaves, each leaflet toothed, sharply pointed at the tip. The husks of their nuts when ripe open into four segments. Shagbark hickories have bark that peels in long shaggy strips, while bitternut hickory bark is tight and ridged. Shagbark trees usually have five leaflets and bitternuts have seven to nine.

Ashes have opposite compound leaves but are easiest to identify in fall by their long, winged fruits that look like canoe paddles. Leaves of white ash, the commonest kind of ash on the old oak dunes, are usually white underneath, and they don't have many teeth at their margins. Black ash is found more often in swamps. Its leaves are much toothier than those of white ash and they are sessile (lack stalks to separate leaf and stem).

Almost everyone, it seems, knows what a maple tree looks like. It has wide, deeply-lobed leaves, odd-looking pairs of winged seeds, and bark that is smooth and gray when the tree is young, scaly, and furrowed in old age.

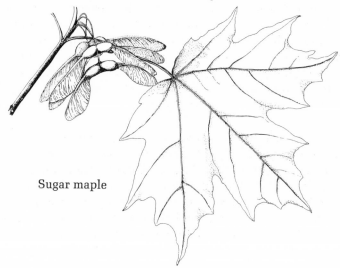

Sugar maple

The lobes of sugar maple leaves are few but larger, with the indentations round and deeper than those of most other maples. In autumn, the leaves turn to blends of red and yellow.

The beech tree is best known by the smooth, pale gray bark it maintains even in its dotage. It is a tree that has tempted people through the ages to carve their initials on its trunk. Pioneer travelers early in the last century often etched trail directions in beech bark for the settlers who would follow them. Beech leaves are elliptical with small but prominent marginal teeth and veins evenly spaced, extending all the way from the midrib to leaf's edge. Beech buds are distinctive, too, long and tapered, and the nuts are triangular, covered with a spiny sort of husk.

Basswoods reach their greatest glory at the dunes on the steep lee slopes of isolated, rich woodland coves that thrive in several locations just behind beaches and young foredunes. They are unique among the hardwood trees that grow in deeper dune forests in their ability, similar to that of cottonwoods, to survive substantial sand burial. They are unable to build dunes, apparently, only because they need more minerals than the sand on an open beach provides. Basswoods are easiest to recognize by their heart-shaped, fine-toothed leaves with uneven bases. Their cream-yellow flowers, opening on summer evenings, have a strong and lovely fragrance. Their fruits are small nutlets that hang on a stalk from large, leafy wings that act like spinning parachutes when they ripen and blow away in autumn.

Tall, slim saplings of sugar maples and tulip trees are common understory trees on the older dunes. They are joined there by black cherries, sassafras, and flowering dogwoods. Shrubbier underbrush includes the familiar witch hazel and choke cherries from more open dunes, along with maple-leaved viburnum, both common and red elderberries, and spicebush. Blueberries are still prominent, though they become scarcer on the very oldest dunes and in moister and less acid soil.

Beech

Chipmunk with beech tree nuts

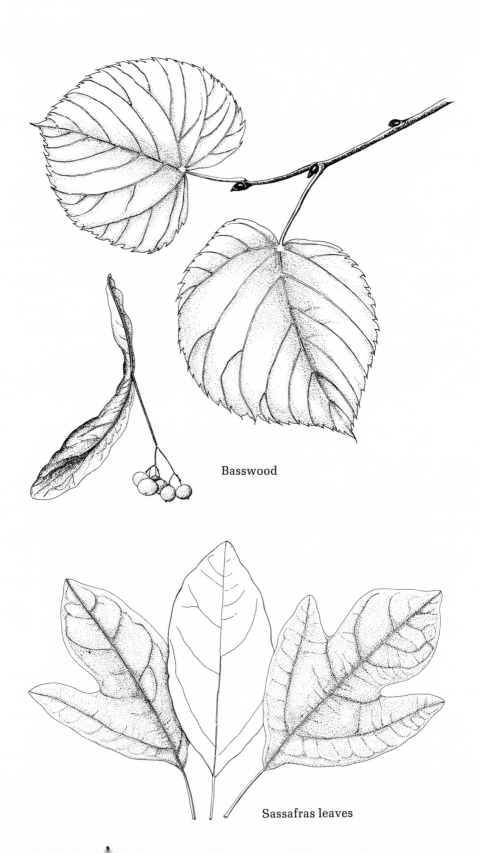

Basswood

Sassafras leaves

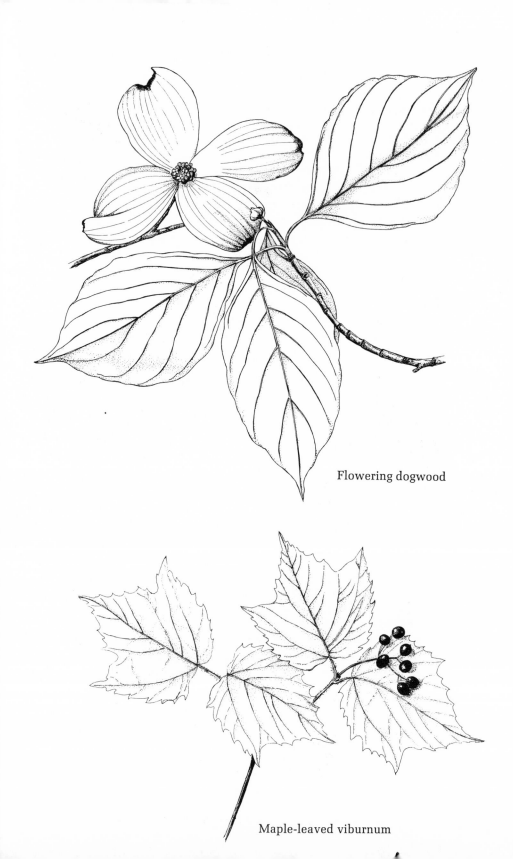

Flowering dogwood

Maple-leaved viburnum

The tulip tree got its name because someone thought its big orange and green flowers looked like the domestic garden tulip. Its leaves, smooth-edged, four-lobed, and deeply notched at the tip, are also unmistakable.

Black cherry trees have dark, scaly "potato chip" bark, with the same broken white horizontal streaks on younger twigs that distinguish its shrubbier cousins, the choke, pin, and sand cherries. Its leaves are long and narrow, blunt-toothed, and its white flowers and dark fruits are strung out in long racemes. Choke cherry fruits grow in long racemes, too, but chokecherry leaves are much wider.

The leaves of sassafras trees, all toothless and broad, come in three types, all of which may occur on the same tree. One has two lobes and looks like a child's mitten. Another has three lobes, and a third is egg-shaped with no separate lobes at all. Budding sassafras leaves would be distinctive in spring, even if they didn't appear before those of most other trees. While still tightly closed, the leaf buds poke stiffly skyward from the topside of their twigs.

Flowering dogwoods are at their most spectacular in late April and early May before their leaves are fully out and when their white blossoms seem almost to float through the understory canopy of deep dune woods. Their leaves, oval and sharp-pointed, toothless, growing opposite each other on their stems, have the same gently curving veins as other dogwoods.

The fruits of flowering dogwood in summer are red. In winter, look for the distinctive buds, shaped like the onion domes of St. Basil's Cathedral in the Kremlin.

Maple-leaved viburnum has broad, three-lobed leaves that do look a little like maple leaves. The undersides of these leaves are velvety and covered with tiny yellow and black dots. Fruits are scarlet at first, then blue-black.

Elderberry bushes have opposite compound leaves, finely-toothed, much like those of ash trees. The white flowers of purple-fruited elderberry grow in dense, flat-topped clusters in June and July. The clusters of red elderberry flowers (white) and fruits (red) are cone-shaped.

Spicebush leaves look a little like dogwood leaves, though their veins are fewer and not as curved. The leaves are toothless and grow alternately along the plant's stems. Spicebush is best known, however, for the perfume given off by its crushed leaves, berries, twigs, and buds.

The deeper shaded woods of the dunes are also host to various berry bushes—black and red raspberries, dewberries, and gooseberries.

Vines give a jungly look to some parts of these woods—virginia creeper mainly, five leaflets to a stalk as compared to three for the also common poison ivy. In the very richest

Spicebush

forest patches, usually those deep, humus-rich pockets near the lake, there is also creeping euonymus, known also as running strawberry bush though it bears no relation to the strawberries you eat with cream and shortcake. Its leaves are egg-shaped, stalkless, finely-toothed, and its twigs, sharply four-sided, trail along the ground among the dense carpet of low flowers. Its red-orange seeds are covered with a prickly-looking, reddish-pink capsule.

The varied and numerous flowers of deep dune woods, like those of the open savannas, can only be comprehensively described in a special field guide.

The earliest spring flower is white or lavender round-lobed hepatica, which blooms in March with shadbush, often before its maroon and green three-lobed leaves have appeared. The leaves grow large in summer, long after the flower is gone, storing nutrients for the next spring's blossoms. Hepatica's

Running strawberry bush

six to ten "petals" are really sepals, or modified leaves. The plant seldom grows more than six inches high.

Other early bloomers (all about the same size as hepatica) are spring beauty (grass-like leaves, pink-veined white petals), violets, both purple and yellow kinds, and rue anemone, with its two or three white flowers growing on slender stalks above a whorl of small leaves.

Trillium (three-petaled flowers with three leaves) and jack in the pulpit soon follow. Jack in the pulpit has three leaflets but is identified easiest by the canopied sheath (the pulpit) which covers and encircles its erect flower stalk (the jack or preacher). Both are about a foot tall when they're in bloom.

Two delicate woodland flowers named for the month in which they bloom are May apples and Canada Mayflower. May apples have broad, deeply lobed leaves above their white flowers and soft yellow fruits. Canada Mayflower, also known as wild lily of the valley, is tiny, seldom more than six inches tall, like many early-blooming woodland flowers. Its wide leaves, pointed at the tips, are heart-shaped at their bases and hug the plant's single stem. Its flowers are white, with two petals and two sepals that grow at the tip of the stem, clustered along a raceme.

Columbine (orange flowers with drooping spurs), bellwort (blossoms yellow, bell-shaped), wild geranium (pink with wide, deeply lobed leaves) and early meadow rue are also among spring bloomers. The meadow rue has drooping, greenish-white flowers and small, three-lobed leaflets on many-stalked stems.

Indian cucumber root, wild sarsaparilla, and sweet cicely follow in June. Wintergreen, another boreal forest plant, a member of the heath family to which bearberry belongs, is one of very few deep woodland flowers to bloom in mid-summer. It has shiny oval leaves that stay green over winter and grow from short, erect branches that extend from creeping stems. The white, waxy flowers are egg-shaped and drooping. Berries are red.

True solomon's seals, both common and downy species, carpet the deep woods. So does the common false solomon's seal, though starry false solomon's seal seldom strays far from open dunes and sunny oak savannas.

Royal fern, cinnamon fern, and Christmas fern appear in deeply-shaded, moist forests along with the familiar bracken of more open woods. Maidenhair fern and ebony spleenwort grow on damp, mossy banks on north slopes of the deepest woods.

Dune Animals

Animals of the forested dunes are mainly those found in most eastern woodlands. Raccoons and skunks are bold camp scavengers. Red and fox squirrels, chipmunks, woodchucks, and cottontail rabbits may also be seen. White-tailed deer and fleeting glimpses of red foxes occasionally startle hikers on dune trails.

Nearly one hundred different species of birds have been identified in the wooded sections of Indiana dune country in a survey by the Chicago Audubon Society. Some, like the scarlet tanager, great-crested flycatcher, and red-eyed vireo, are hard to see because they feed from the tops of the tallest trees. The vireo is a constant talker, though. You can hear him calling his name, over and over, always very fast, all through your day in the woods. One studious observer, L. de Kiriline, writing for *Audubon Magazine* in 1954, said he listened to a particular vireo repeat its song 22,197 times in a single day.

Common birds in the lower tree branches of dune woods include five kinds of woodpeckers—flickers, red-bellied and red-headed woodpeckers, downy and hairy woodpeckers. Blue jays also venture below tree tops. Their raucous call serves to warn other woodland animals when human visitors are approaching. The bright red and black warblers called redstarts (females are black and yellow) are easier to spot than most warblers in leafy woods. Chickadees, which prefer to nest in pines if any are available, venture in flocks among the lower branches of deciduous woods in winter, along with red- and white-breasted nuthatches.

Birds that favor underbrush and thickets are the long-tailed, reddish-hued brown thrasher, golden-crowned and ruby-crowned kinglets, and cardinals.

Ground feeders include towhees, robins, wood thrushes, and ovenbirds. All four of these birds are highly voluble, singing loudly from their perches in low tree branches. The towhee's song sounds like the first three notes of the George M. Cohan song from World War I, "Over There." The Roger Tory Peterson field guide claims it says "Drink your tea." The robin's songs are long and complicated, punctuated into phrases of two or three notes each. The wood thrush song is also long, with a tone that sounds like a flute. Ovenbirds scream "teacher, teacher, teacher" incessantly, with the accent on the second syllable.

Eastern forest woodland is among the richest of small animal habitats, and the oak woods at Indiana dunes is no exception. Elliott Rowland Downing, who wrote a charming book in the 1920s called *A Naturalist in the Great Lakes Region,* told of a Miss Nell Saunders who "took an animal census one midsummer and found in a mixed area of swale, cottonwoods, and oaks 16 million animals to the acre. Three-quarters of a million on the ground stratum, three million on the herbaceous plants, ten million on the shrubs, and the remainder on the trees."

Victor Shelford, the zoologist who did the first studies of animal ecosystems at the dunes, called the open savannas of black oak dunes "the ant lion association" and the deeper woods a "hylodes association" for its great abundance of tree frogs.

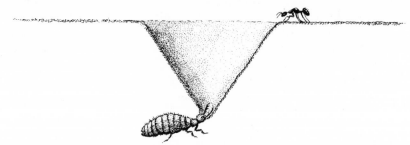

Ant lion larva in its pit waiting for prey

The conical holes of the ant-lions can be spotted by careful observers on patches of open, sandy ground between the trees. The pits these predatory little insects build are usually about two inches wide. Ant lion larvae lie in wait at the bottom of the pits for other unwary insects to drop in. If you stick a grass blade into the hole, the larva may fasten its jaws onto it and you can bring it out of its lair for a closer look.

The deeper woods with its abundance of decaying logs makes a home for earthworms, various snails and salamanders, millipedes and centipedes as well as crickets and tree frogs, the green tiger beetle, and nearly a dozen kinds of butterflies.

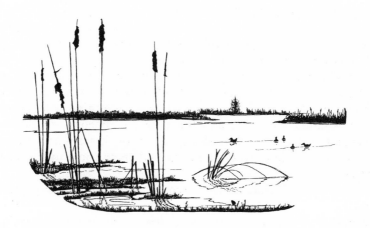

WETLANDS

Between the rows of high, dry hills of sand in Indiana dune country are ponds where wood ducks hide, and long, low ribbons of marsh where cattails wave in gentle breezes and water lilies float at ease on the still water's surface.

There are swamp forests, too, damp, dark, primeval-looking places. And there are bogs, exotic isolated worlds only a few hundred acres in size, with plants that eat mosquitoes and floating mats of moss where a person can literally walk, dryshod, on water. The mats eventually become strong enough to support whole floating forests of tamarack trees.

Some of the marshes evolved from shallow backwaters of Dune Creek or the Little Calumet River. Others were once lakes or ponds, born when wind scoured dunes down to the water table, like the interdunal ponds behind the foredunes on West Beach, or when fast-dropping lake levels in past centuries left long, shallow lagoons between high beach ridges. The Great Marsh, strung out between Dune Creek and Long Lake north of U. S. 12, is one such ancient lagoon.

The plants and animals that live in a lake or along its edges are bound to die eventually, sinking to the bottom where bacteria transform them into a rich organic soup.

If a lake has fast enough drainage, it may carry away enough of these deposits to maintain itself. If drainage is slow, however, the decayed remains will pile up along with layers of rain-washed sediment, and the lake will become shallower. When that happens, the cattails and reeds, grasses and sedges that once made only a border extend their roots ever closer to the pool's center.

Red-winged blackbirds arrive to stake out nesting territories on the cattail and reed stalks. Spatterdock and other water lilies spread their broad leaves over the remaining patches of open water, and the lake becomes a marsh.

The appeal of a marsh is not as immediate as that of a sunny beach or a woodland carpeted with wildflowers. But the life in a marsh is more complex and abundant than that of almost any other habitat. It begins to stir early in spring, while upland woods and sandy shores are still frozen in the grip of winter. Bullfrogs and spring peepers begin their annual chorus while skins of ice still cover the ponds, and the light green shoots of cattails sprout in the first week of March.

There are two kinds of cattails in dune marshes. Common cattails have wider leaves, and the two parts of the tubular, brown, flowering stalk touch each other. Narrow-leaved cattails have leaves that explain their name and a section of green stem that separates the two parts of the brown, flowering spike.

Bur-reeds, grasses, and sedges also help bring the marsh to life in early spring. The bur-reeds have long, slender leaves with fruits growing on separate stalks in dense, bur-like clusters. The grass you're most likely to see is bluejoint or northern reed grass, a close relative of the sandreed grass of foredunes. The sedges include marsh sedge (*Carex stricta* is the Latin name) and bulrushes (woolgrass, chairmaker's rush, and soft-stemmed or great bulrush). By summer the plants in a marsh cover every inch of ground and water space, and the animal activity is ceaseless. Water striders and water boatmen skate over the pond surface, while banded watersnakes chase green frogs from the floating leaves of water lilies.

Dragonflies and damselflies dart about in search of mosquitoes and other flying insects. To tell them apart, you must wait until they stop to rest on a leaf or reed stalk. Damselflies fold their wings while dragonflies spread them wide.

If you're out early in the morning, you may see a weasel sliding down a muddy bank into the water or a muskrat scurrying about to gather twigs for his conical house. Raccoons probe the shrubby edges of the marsh and dip paws into the pools for dinners of clams or crayfish.

The birds of dune wetlands are the herons (great blue herons and green herons are the most plentiful) and dabbling ducks. To watch a heron fishing, stepping daintily along in slow motion while waiting for the moment to strike, is to watch grace personified. Mallards are more comical to human eyes, standing on their heads in the water to nibble on underwater pondweeds with only their tufted rear ends poking above the surface.

Other dabblers in dune marshes, the ducks that are vegetarians rather than fish-eaters, are blue- and green-winged teals and bright colored wood ducks, with their odd habit of nesting in trees.

Coots, black with white bills, are often found nearby. They are duck-sized birds that walk and fly clumsily like barnyard chickens.

Great blue heron

Water lilies with their flat, floating leaves blossom in May or June and keep their flowers all summer, making bright splashes of color on the ponds and providing warm, sunny perches for small frogs and various insects. The undersides of their leaves are home to tiny sponges, water mites, and the eggs of beetles, snails, and damselflies.

Commonest of dune water lilies are yellow spatterdock, white water lily, and watershield, with smaller leaves than those of the other two and tiny, dull-purple flowers.

Another group of showy marsh plants grow in shallow water near the pond edges and have leaves that angle above the water rather than floating on its surface. Pickerelweed, with its bright purple flowers on tall spikes, is among this group. So are arrowheads, also known as duck potatoes because of their edible, tuberous roots.

Arrowheads have small, white, three-petaled flowers and leaves that vary widely in shape from plant to plant. The commonest is deeply notched with sharply-pointed tips. The leaf veins extend in three directions toward the three-pointed edges of the "arrowhead." Grass-leaved arrowhead, as its name implies, has long, slender, grasslike leaves. Pickerelweed leaves are similar to those of common arrowhead but broader and more rounded, and their veins extend all in one direction from base to tip.

Other plants that thrive in shallow water or muddy banks include marsh smartweed, with long, slim spikes of pink flowers, and swamp candles, a yellow-flowered loosestrife, its blossoms also on long spikes.

The tiny green dots that float on the surface of most marshes may look at first like algae. More likely, they are various species of duckweed, the smallest flowering plants in the world.

The more heavily populated a marsh becomes, the faster its bottom fills with organic matter. As it grows shallower over the years, shrubs like willow, buttonbush, and black chokeberry that once were scattered only sparsely among the cattails, begin to form impenetrable thickets. The noisy yellowthroat appears to sing its incessant "witcherly, witcherly" from their branches.

There are more species of willows in dune wetlands than on foredunes and blowouts, but they have the same general characteristics—alternate leaves, usually longer than wide; long, furry catkins in spring; single coverings or scales on their buds.

Chokeberries have fine-toothed, elliptic leaves with tiny black glands on the tip of each tooth. There are also small

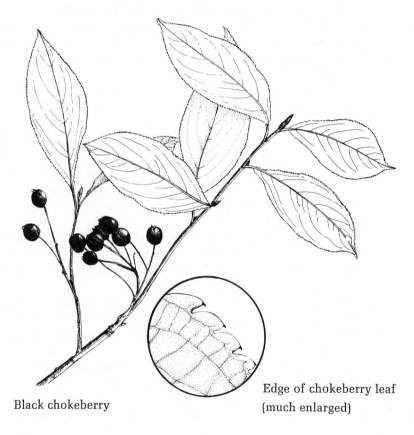

Black chokeberry

Edge of chokeberry leaf
(much enlarged)

raised glands on the midribs (visible without a hand lens if you squint a bit). The white flowers and black berries grow in clusters.

Buttonbush has smooth-edged leaves that grow opposite or in whorls of three or four around the stem. Its flowers are white, small, tubular, and clustered in tightly-packed, round "buttons," or balls.

The flowers that grow at the edge of the open marsh gradually disappear as more and more shrubs grow to block their shade. The water becomes even shallower and eventually rich enough in minerals to support trees as well as shrubs. When red maples and sourgum, yellow birch and pin oaks grow large enough to spread a canopy over the wetlands, they cease to fit the name of marsh and become a swamp forest.

Red maples have leaves three-lobed, each lobe roughly triangular, with shallow-toothed edges.

Pin oaks have five-to-seven-lobed leaves, shiny and sharp-pointed, and lower branches that, unlike those of most other oaks, droop down. The lowest branches often touch the ground.

Sourgum, more common in bottomland forests of the South than here in the Midwest, turns a bright red early in fall when most other trees are still green. Its leaves are simple, alternate, oval in shape, very shiny and usually smooth-edged.

Yellow birch is a northern plant, nearing its southern range limit at the dunes. It has finely-toothed leaves with round or heart-shaped bases. On each leaf's underside, you can see tufts of fine hairs in the axils of the veins. The tree's bark is a yellowish-bronze and peels in strips like the bark of white birch. There are scattered groves of white birches at the dunes, too. They are able to grow in a wider range of habitats than the swamp-loving yellow birch.

Skunk cabbage is usually the first sign of spring in a swamp forest, poking the tip of its hooded sheath, mottled green or purplish-brown, above snow in February. Tiny, yellowish blossoms on a round knob called a spadix nestle inside

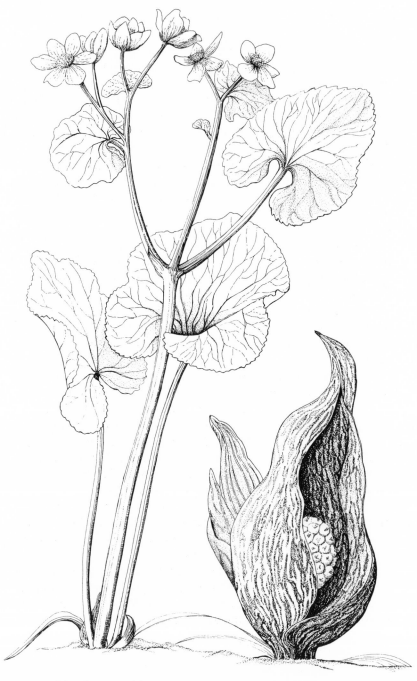

Marsh marigold   Skunk cabbage

the sheltering hood. The plant's broad leaves, coiled at first and unfolding only gradually, are last to appear. They have a strong, fetid odor when crushed.

Marsh marigolds bloom in April and often last until June. They are also known as cowslip and bear no resemblance at all to domestic marigolds. They are actually members of the buttercup family, and their shiny yellow petals (really sepals, or modified leaves), while larger than other buttercups, otherwise look much like them.

Jewelweed, with bright orange or yellow blossoms and leaves that glisten silver underwater, is everywhere. Only slightly less abundant are the great wild irises called blue flag, yellow swamp buttercups, and delicate pink swamp roses.

At least six kinds of fern thrive in swamp forests at the dunes—royal ferns, cinnamon ferns, marsh, sensitive, Christmas, and grape ferns. There are also more tiny boreal plants in this cool, damp environment than any other place in the area. Goldthread, starflower, and bunchberry are all survivors from Ice Age times.

Goldthread has bright yellow runners that creep along aboveground, white flowers, and shiny, dark, three-parted evergreen leaves. Starflowers have sharply-pointed, starlike, white blossoms on long stems above a whorl of green leaves. Bunchberries, tiny herbaceous members of the dogwood family, have four-petaled white flowers (actually modified leaves) followed by red berries in midsummer. Their leaves, in a whorl beneath the flowers, have the same curved veins that other dogwoods have.

Bogs are Ice Age relics, too, found often adjacent to swamp forests. They are fairly common in the more recently glaciated landscape of northern Wisconsin, Michigan's Upper Peninsula, and Maine, but are rare this far south. Indiana Dunes National Lakeshore is fortunate to have two within its borders—Cowles Bog west of Mineral Springs Road in Dune Acres and Pinhook Bog south of Michigan City. Cowles Bog is off limits entirely to visitors at the moment. The National Lakeshore staff hopes eventually to build a path to it and a boardwalk across it. Pinhook is accessible only on special guided tours with park naturalists.

Bogs are like marshes in that they develop when vegetation fills in space once occupied by clear water. They are different in that they have virtually no drainage, a condition that creates highly acid conditions and a low oxygen content that hinders decay. (The water of bogs is usually brown; that of marshes tends to have a greenish tinge). The well-preserved body of a man two thousand years old was found by peat cutters in a bog in Denmark in 1950. More than a hundred similarly ancient and barely decayed bodies have since been found in other European bogs. No such dramatic discoveries have been made in the bogs at Indiana Dunes, but scientists have learned a great deal about past climates in the area from the different kinds of pollen preserved at various depths in bog muck. By drilling down to bedrock and extracting soil samples at different levels, they should theoretically be able, with the aid of Carbon-14 dating techniques, to produce a kind of almanac dating back to the glacier's retreat, about 12,000 B. C.

The acidity and the nutrient-poor quality of bogwater also produces plants quite different from those that grow nearby in swamps and marshes. Much of the water in bogs is inaccessible to plants, so the species that grow there have adaptations for conserving moisture similar to those of desert plants.

Many of them are heaths, a particular group of evergreens with succulent leaves designed to conserve fresh rainwater. Among the commonest heaths in dune bogs are leatherleaf, blueberries, and cranberries. Bog rosemary, more widespread in bogs farther north, is found in small numbers at Pinhook.

The leaves of leatherleaf are long and slim, covered with small dots, and grow alternately along its stems. The flowers are small, white, and bell-shaped.

Two kinds of creeping cranberry bushes, large and small, are found at Pinhook Bog. Both are close relatives of the blueberries that grow in dune sand but are also found in the bogs. The leaves of both cranberries grow alternately on long, trailing stems and have white or pale undersides.

Those of small cranberry are egg-shaped or triangular, pointed, with rolled edges. The leaves of large cranberry are wedge-shaped to round, blunt-tipped, flat or with slightly rolled edges. The flowers of both cranberries are pink, and their fruits, sometimes bigger than the leaves, look like the cranberries you buy in the grocery store.

Bog rosemary leaves are much narrower than those of leatherleaf, and its drooping flowers are white tinged with pink.

Sphagnum moss floats on the surface of the ponds in most bogs, including the two at the dunes. Wispy and stringlike, it looks very different from most other mosses. If you squeeze a handful of it, a surprising amount of water will pour out. It can absorb more than eighteen times its weight in water.

Sphagnum may eventually fill in a bog from the surface down, rather than filling the pond in from the bottom as do marsh plants. It becomes strong enough at some point to support the root systems of large trees. If you jump up and down on a mature sphagnum mat, you can see trees shake from the reverberation a hundred yards away.

The most important tree in Indiana Dune bogs is the tamarack, a conifer that looks like other conifers in summer but turns yellow and loses its needles in autumn like an oak or a maple. Tamarack needles are short, blue-green, and grow in clusters. Its cones are small and round, reminding one of carved wooden roses.

White pines are scattered throughout the bogs, more of them at Pinhook than at Cowles.

Bog or dwarf birch is another bog specialty. Its leaves are wider near the tip and not so sharply pointed as those of other birches. The leaves are toothed, pale green, sometimes white underneath, and their twigs are hairy. They are also shrubbier than other birches, seldom growing more than nine feet tall.

Tamarack

One of the biggest disadvantages of bogs, from a visitor's point of view, is that they are almost always bordered by thickets of poison sumac. This is one plant definitely worth learning to identify, for it causes a rash even more virulent than that of poison ivy. Its leaves are compound, toothless, with seven to thirteen pointed leaflets. Its bark is smooth and dark with white streaks that often encircle the trunk. Its buds and twigs, unlike those of other sumacs, are hairless. Its fruits in winter are white.

Poison sumac

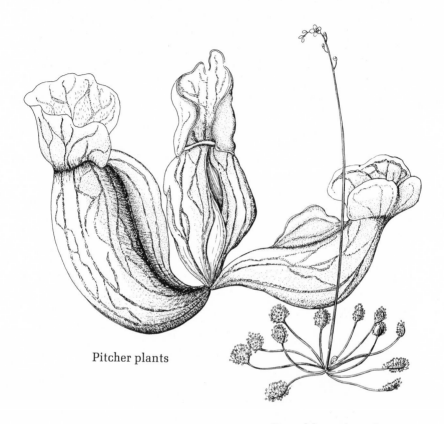

Pitcher plants

Round-leaved sundew

There are rare, orange-fringed orchids, pink lady's slippers, grass pink, and rose pogonia in the dune bogs, with flowers much smaller and more delicate-looking than hothouse orchids. Other flowers include grass-of-Parnassus, with white, five-petaled, green-veined flowers and broad, smooth-edged leaves at the base of their stems; and bog buckbean, distinguished by its three-parted leaves and stalks of frosty-white, fuzzy-bearded petals.

The most dramatic bog plants by far, though, are the carnivorous pitcher plants and sundews. The heavily-veined red or green leaves of pitcher plants are folded to make a kind of cup or pitcher usually half-filled with water. The flaring lips are lined with downward-pointing bristles that help trap insects. The plant produces special enzymes which are mixed with the water in the pitcher to dissolve the captured insects and convert them into nitrogen. The nodding, rose-like, brownish-red flower grows from a separate stalk.

Sundews, both the round-leaved and spatulate-leaved types, are abundant at Pinhook, scattered at Cowles. They are tiny, seldom more than six inches high, with red, sticky stems and red, sticky leaves in a rosette at their base. The sticky substance helps this plant capture and digest its animal food. Flowers, white or pink in a one-sided cluster, are inconspicuous.

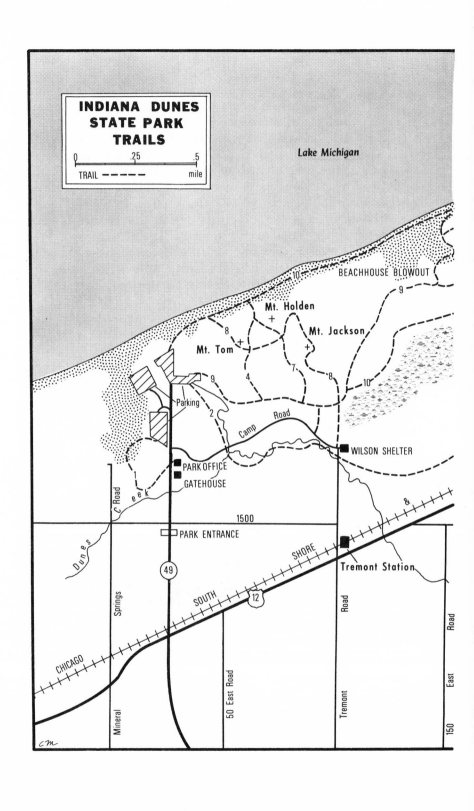

INDIANA DUNES
STATE PARK
TRAILS

0   .25   .5

TRAIL — — — — —   mile

Lake Michigan

BEACHHOUSE BLOWOUT

10

9

Mt. Holden
+

8

Mt. Jackson
+

Mt. Tom
+

9

4   7

8

10

Parking

2   Camp   Road

WILSON SHELTER

1

PARK OFFICE

GATEHOUSE

C Road

e e k

Dunes

1500

PARK ENTRANCE

8

SHORE

49

Tremont Station

SOUTH   12

Springs

CHICAGO

Mineral

50 East Road

Tremont   Road

East   Road

150

cm

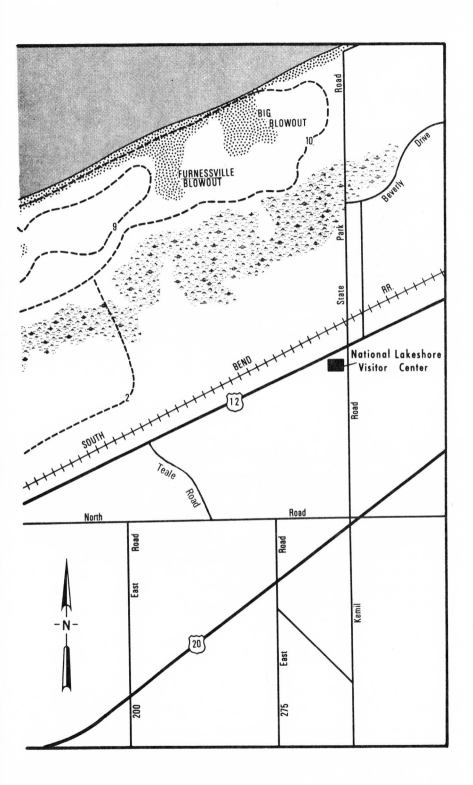

BIG BLOWOUT

FURNESSVILLE BLOWOUT

10

9

2

Park Road

State

Beverly Drive

RR.

National Lakeshore
Visitor Center

Kemil Road

SOUTH BEND

Teale Road

North Road

East Road

East Road

200

275 East

12

20

-N-

TRAILS IN INDIANA DUNES
STATE PARK

Access: Take Indiana Route 49 north from Interstate 94 three miles to road's end at the park entrance.

Description: There are 16½ miles of trails in the state park. They form an elaborate network of loops that offer hikers the choice of round trip strolls as short as a quarter-mile or as long as seven miles.

In two days of exploring the park leisurely on foot, you can sample almost every sort of habitat the area has to offer. There are trails that wind gently on flat ground through hardwood forests and white pine groves, around swamps and

124

across marshes on sturdy wooden bridges. And for hikers who like physical challenges as well as scenery, there are paths that climb at 30-degree angles up the steep sides of sandy dunes. Thirty degrees is said to be the angle of sand at rest. The sand beneath your feet on a walk up one of these dunes is not at rest, however. It is busy carrying your feet back downhill half a step for every step forward you attempt. Hurrying only makes things worse. If you've backpacked in the Rockies, though, or even in the Appalachians, even these climbs will be a breeze for you. None is longer than 64 yards (about one-seventh of a mile) from base to summit.

Because erosion progresses quickly on sandy soil, undermining the roots of dune flowers, grasses, and trees, park officials request that hikers restrict exploration to established trails. They also ask that pets be kept on leashes, that campers camp only in designated campgrounds, and that fires be built only in the enclosed grills designed for that purpose. If you didn't bring a camp stove or charcoal briquets for cooking, you may purchase firewood at the ranger station.

Twigs and fallen branches should not be gathered for kindling. Left to decay naturally, they enrich the soil that enables the forest to replenish itself.

Berry-picking is allowed in moderation, but it's a good idea to leave a generous share for the park birds and other animals. They'll spread the seeds around to make an even more bountiful crop for the future.

Flower- and fern-gathering is prohibited. So is littering.

Facilities available at the park (other than trails) include two campgrounds, (one restricted to large groups that make reservations in advance), picnic areas, pumps and fountains for drinking water, both flush and primitive toilets (the flush toilets are closed in winter), a dumping station for recreational vehicles, and electrical hookups. There are showers, a snack bar, and two grocery stores in summer (one on the beach road, one in the campground), a swimming beach with lifeguards, and a park naturalist for special guided tours and occasional evening slide shows.

Trails on state park maps are numbered 1, 2, 4, 7, 8, 9, and 10. Presumably there were once trails numbered 3, 5, and 6, but they are no longer there and none of the park workers now can remember when or where they existed.

For information, write Indiana Dunes State Park c/o Superintendent, M. R., Box 322, Chesterton, IN. 46304. Telephone: (219) 926-1215.

Trail 1 (1 mile) begins directly across from the park superintendent's office on the west side of the road that leads from the park entrance to the beach. It heads west, north, and then east in a half circle to end at a parking lot adjacent to the beach road just south of the park's grocery store.

This trail skirts the south edge of and then passes through an area where a fire in 1969 raged out of control, burning some ten acres before it could be stopped.

The blackened stumps of pines and oak trees are all but obliterated now by the dense thicket of shrubs and vines and the bright blooms of a host of wildflowers. The supply of fresh red raspberries seems inexhaustible.

Most of us, raised on Smokey the Bear's wise warnings against the careless use of matches, forget that fire can also start from natural causes, like lightning, and that it played an important part in forest ecosystems long before there were enough people around to make much of a difference. The dense thicket of shrubs, for instance, means a constant supply of fresh, green woody shoots, the very sort of meal savored most by whitetail deer, bobwhite quail, and cottontail rabbits. Researchers have found that a severe burn can produce as many as twenty-four thousand new woody shoots per acre, compared to only a few hundred in deep woods.

If you visit a fire-scorched area for several years in a row, you will see drastic change take place, especially in the first decade, in kinds of plant and animal life found there. A formal record of such change is being kept for another burn area in the dunes, a 55-acre tract intersected by the Li-Co-Ki-

We Horse Trail on National Lakeshore land.

In the first summer or two, there are mostly grasses and sun-loving herbaceous plants like goldenrod and sunflowers and hairy puccoon (many of the same plants you see on foredunes near the beach). Sparrows dine there on seeds, and woodpeckers nest in the dead hollow trees.

Shrubs like witch hazel and chokecherry come next, along with raspberry bushes, catbirds, quail, and deer. (More than 150 species of birds and mammals, including humans, are said to love raspberries. None of this, of course, means that nature needs any help from human fire starters.)

Eventually there are young black oaks and the saplings of sassafras. When they grow tall enough to spread a solid canopy, the woods will look again much as it did before the fire struck.

The last few hundred yards of your hike on Trail 1 takes you through a sandy black oak woods to the parking lot.

Trail 2 (3 miles) begins at the southeast corner of a parking lot on the east side of the road between the beach and park entrance. It follows Dune Creek south and then east for a mile, then passes through a mature hardwood forest (a 1½-mile segment) before turning north for a half-mile and crossing a marsh to join Trail 10.

The first half-mile of trail follows a narrow strip of flat ground between a steep wooded dune and the west bank of Dune Creek. The creek is narrow and fast-moving on this section. Spring beauty and rue anemone bloom on the hillsides in April and May, and patches of maidenhair fern appear among the mosses on the creek's bank.

The trail heads south across a road leading to the campground from the park entrance road and then meanders east as the creek bends east, moving sluggishly now in a wider bed. The trail crosses another road, this one leading south to a group youth campsite, before entering a zone of second growth lowland forest.

The land here was clearcut sometime before it was deeded

to the state for a park in 1925, and attempts were made, apparently without success, to drain it for farming. Small wooden bridges mark spots where the trail crosses ditches built for that purpose.

The trees in this woods are mainly black cherry, sassafras, and red maple, with some big tooth aspen and beech just west of the road that heads south from Wilson Shelter. They are all small and look younger than park records show them to be. Their growth may have been slowed by periodic flooding of Dune Creek over the years. A great deal of sunlight filters through, so underbrush is heavy. Four or five species of goldenrod flourish along the path.

At one point the trail passes along the south edge of a swamp pond, a wide backwater of the creek. Redheaded woodpeckers, drawn by insects that live in the numerous dead trees, are abundant. Buttonbush grows along the pond margin.

When you cross the road that leads south from Wilson Shelter, continuing east on Trail 2, you may have a sense of stepping into the future. The woods you have just walked through won't look like this for another half a century.

Giant beeches, red oak, and white ash trees spread their leafy branches high above your head, making the forest floor cool and shadowy in the middle of a summer's day. A ninety-foot tulip tree, felled by disease or a storm in its vulnerable old age, sprawls along the ground north of the trail beside an ox-bow meander of the creek. Jewelweed, a plant with flaring-lipped, bell-shaped orange blossoms, takes advantage of the patch of sunlight that reaches the ground where the tulip tree once stood.

Most of the wildflowers in this forest are those like hepatica that bloom early in spring before there are leaves on the trees. The birds are those more likely to be heard than seen, for they spend most of their days in the treetops. An occasional bright flash of red may signal the presence of a scarlet tanager.

The ground becomes drier and the vegetation changes subtly as the trail leaves the creek and continues east through an upland forest on a gentle ridge of the Tolleston beach era (see chapter 1 for more about geology). Sugar maples, black and white oaks, and an occasional shagbark hickory become part of the canopy forest. Young sugar maples, tulip trees, and spicebush make an understory along with gooseberry and elderberry bushes.

After 1½ miles, the trail turns north and crosses a marsh in the late stages of transition to a swamp forest. Willow and chokeberry thickets cover the expanse of shallow water, keeping out the sun that nourished waterlilies and pickerelweed in an earlier stage of succession.

Pin oak and red maple trees are beginning now, in their turn, to keep sun from the thickets of shrubs.

The east branch of Dune Creek has its beginnings in this marsh.

Trail 2 ends north of it in another upland forest where it joins Trail 10 about a mile and a half east of Wilson Shelter.

Trail 4 (¾ mile) heads north from a playground and covered pavilion in the campground, winding gradually uphill in low ravines between sandy black oak dunes to junction with Trail 8 on the east slope of Mt. Tom.

This whole area, crisscrossed by Trails 4, 7, and 8, has the highest dunes in the entire State Park and National Lakeshore. The three most spectacular peaks in the dune complex are Mt. Tom (elevation 771 feet or 192 feet above the beach), Mt. Holden (elevation 763 feet), and Mt. Jackson (elevation 755 feet). Viewed from these hilltops, the surrounding countryside gives one a real feeling for the complexity of dune country landscape.

Trail 4 continues north and slightly east from Mt. Tom along a route about halfway up the lee slope of a long dune ridge. The bottom of the slope on the east side of the trail is a mesic hardwood cove, a rarity in dune country because of its dark, humus-rich soil and the great variety of trees able to flourish there—basswoods, sugar maple and red oak, white ash, tulip trees, shagbark, and bitternut hickory.

Leaf litter from these trees, combined with organic matter that washes down the slopes with rainfall, is able to decay at leisure on the cove floor, safely protected from wind by the high wooded dune that separates it from the beach.

Trail 4 is a favorite haunt of birders during spring migration, because your vantage point halfway up the slope lets you look straight into the tree canopy where dozens of tiny warblers are sure to be darting about.

The flowers in this wood are best in spring, too. Among them are hepatica, running strawberry bush, wild lily of the valley, downy solomon's seal, columbine, bellwort, and jack-in-the-pulpit.

Trail 4 ends at junction with Trail 7, at the northeast end of the long dune ridge, behind a low foredune just above the beach.

Trail 7 (1 mile) winds gradually uphill from the western edge of the group camp (a cluster of buildings just east of the main campground), and then begins a steeper ascent up heavily eroded dunes before it crosses Trail 8 on the south slopes of Mt. Holden.

Trail 7 is probably the least painful route, in terms of physical exertion, to travel over the high dunes from the campground to the beach without missing out on the great variety of terrain contained in the high dune country.

From the Trail 8 junction it follows the edge of a grassy, open meadow near the top of a long dune ridge that runs northwest to southeast from the lake. It enters the woods on the west slopes of these ridges to overlook, from a different perspective, the same deep hardwood cove you saw from Trail 4. Trail 7 joins Trail 4 at the edge of this deep woodland on a foredune just above the beach. Aromatic sumac and wild pasture roses are unusually abundant on the shrubby margin of this particular foredune.

Trail 8 (3¾ miles) begins at Wilson Shelter and Picnic Area, half a mile by road east of the main campground. It heads north, crossing a marsh on a long wooden footbridge. This is the same marsh you crossed on Trail 2, the marsh in which the east branch of Dune Creek is born, a part of the long ribbon of marsh and swamp land that continues with few interruptions past the Cowles Bog area in Dune Acres all the way to Long Lake in the West Beach section of the National Lakeshore.

Water lilies and pickerelweed still dominate this open, sunny part of the marsh, though willow thickets have begun to creep in from the edges.

The trail continues north uphill from the marsh into a forest of black and white oaks. The white blossoms of shadbush are particularly spectacular on this trail in March, when most of the forest is still a wintery brown. Fall-blooming witch hazel extends the flowering season at the other end of summer.

Blueberry bushes, two kinds of false solomon's seal, royal and sensitive fern can be found along the trail in this woods. The commonest flowers in midsummer seem to be lyre-leaved rock cress (known locally as sand cress), dwarf dandelion, and deep blue Iris-like spiderwort.

Trail 8 crosses Trails 10 and 9 then begins a half mile ascent that gets gradually steeper as you approach the top of Mt. Holden.

From Mt. Holden, the trail heads west, continually up and down dunes in a route designed to delight the physically fit and frustrate everyone else.

After climbing Mt. Tom at the steepest angle possible, Trail 8 heads down to the beach. Sand reed grass, little bluestem prairie grass, and scattered thickets of sand cherry dot the slope. A small grove of jack pines appears halfway down, mixed with common juniper and tangled mats of bearberry.

The foredunes at the foot of Mt. Tom are covered with marram grass, cottonwood, and sand cherry. Erosion has carved steep sand cliffs above the beach.

Trail 9 (3¾ miles) begins at the northeast corner of a parking lot on the east side of the road that leads from the park entrance to the beach. (Trail 2 begins at the southeast corner of the same parking lot).

It heads east through a forest of black and white oaks, young dogwoods and chokecherries, for a quarter-mile to the campground.

If you walk across the north edge of the campground, at the base of the high dune, you can pick up the trail again (watch for the sign) at the campground's eastern edge.

NOTE: Maps distributed at the state park entrance show Trail 9 following the dune ridge top north of the campground and crossing Trails 7 and 8 just north of the group camp. Use of this part of the trail is being discouraged, however, because of erosion damage from overuse of the dune ridge.

The trail crosses the southern boundary of the group camp to junction with Trail 10 and then heads northeast toward Beachhouse Blowout across gently rolling dune hills in a sandy black oak/blueberry woods.

This kind of forest is the most typical of all habitats in that part of the dunes that dates from the Tolleston beach era, land that was bare sand some eight thousand years ago.

Lupines, sand cress, spiderwort, and phlox are among the commonest of flowers along most of the trail route. The woods become more open as you get closer to Beachhouse Blowout and the lakeshore, and tall grasses and sedges become a more important part of the landscape. Starry false solomon's seal marches up bare sand strips of dunes converted by children into natural slides. The flowers change, too. Yellow-flowered puccoon and birdsfoot violet grow in bigger patches on the ground in early summer, black-eyed susans, thimbleweed, goats' rue and fern-leaved false foxglove in July.

The view alters suddenly and drastically when you reach the edge of Beachhouse Blowout and gaze out toward the lake over its deep grassy bowl, studded with cottonwoods. There was once a large tree graveyard in this blowout, a gaunt ghost forest left standing in the dessicated air when a moving dune passed over it. Most of these trees have fallen now, and little is left to see of them but the decaying piles of black wood chunks on the ground. They are said to have been mostly white pines.

Trail 9 skirts the southern rim of Beachhouse Blowout and passes along the edge of a hardwood grove on the blowout's east side. The trees in this grove are mainly hop hornbeam, basswood, red osier dogwood, and black oak.

The path continues east on a pine- and juniper-clad ridgetop that separates open foredunes from a steep, wooded lee slope covered with basswoods and the vines of virginia creeper. The stages of plant succession that led Dr. Henry Chandler Cowles to form his theories about ecology may be demarcated more clearly along the stretch of land visible from this trail than almost anywhere else in the dunes.

The trail follows this ridge for almost a mile to Furnessville Blowout before turning back east to make a loop inland through another sandy black oak woods to rejoin the main part of the trail just south of Beachhouse Blowout.

Trail 10 (5½ miles) is the long distance champion of state park trails, although it's easier to navigate than Trail 8 because almost all of it is on flat ground. It begins at the pavilion and bath house and heads east along the beach for 3½ miles before turning inland near the park's eastern border and heading west through an upland black oak and mixed hardwood forest. Trail 10 ends at junction with Trails 8 and 9 just north of Wilson Shelter.

The strip of trail that follows the beach is among the best places in the park to play at ecological detective. One can splash along the water's edge, squishing toes in the wet sand and looking for the tiny insects and crustaceans that live there. Or one can make a game of finding and identifying the handful of plant species hardy enough to survive on the wind-tossed beach (see chapter 2 for descriptions and illustrations).

There are six blowouts to explore along the way, the three

big ones (Beachhouse, Furnessville, and Big Blowout) shown on official State Park maps, plus three smaller ones, carved partly by human traffic but mainly by a decade of high lake levels at the dunes since the official maps were made.

The long years of high water have also made grassy foredunes rarer than they once were and thus a bigger treat to find. A few new ones began to build late in the summer of 1976 as water levels started to drop again, but you will notice a few places where waves have cut cliffs all the way back to the edge of black oak woods. (See chapter 3 for more detail on foredunes).

The first blowout is still just a shallow trough of bare, sand worn down by hikers immediately east of the pine grove that borders the road east of the beachhouse and pavilion. (See chapter 4 for more detail about blowouts).

A black oak woods interspersed with pines lies behind a narrow strip of foredunes east of this blowout.

The second blowout, also still small, cuts inland from the beach a few yards east of the junction of Trail 10 with Trails 4 and 7. Tufts of marram have already begun to cover the bare sand, so this blowout may become stabilized before it has a chance to grow bigger.

That's what apparently happened to a small bowl that almost became a blowout just west of Beachhouse Blowout. A new marram grass and cottonwood foredune has formed in front of this bowl, and the steep slope behind it is now covered with red cedar, black oak saplings, sand cherry, and little bluestem grass.

Beachhouse Blowout is really a pair of blowouts separated by a long forested dune that runs perpendicular to the lake. The westernmost blowout of the pair is a vast complex of hills and valleys. Some of the valleys are still bare sand, but several are carpeted with little bluestem, marram, and sand reed grasses. Cottonwoods are abundant, but the sand cherry so prominent on other foredunes and blowouts is relatively scarce in this one.

The easternmost blowout is now almost entirely closed off from the beach by a new foredune. Some time before that foredune was created, however, wind dug the sand of this blowout down to the water table, and a small intredunal pond still survives there. Juniper covers the slope on the west side of this blowout, and cottonwoods make a row through its damp, low center.

East of the Beachhouse Blowout twins is a long, narrow stretch of little bluestem foredunes. Wave-cut cliffs have long since eroded the marram grass that once made a buffer zone between the little bluestem and the lake.

A grove of jack pines reaching down to the beach east of the patch of foredunes makes a nice place to stop for lunch or to seek shelter from sun on a hot summer day. A forest of tall white pines stretches out behind the foredunes east of the jack pine grove.

Furnessville Blowout is an open grassy sort of place, dotted here and there with spires of red cedar, some common juniper, and cottonwoods. Like the Beachhouse Blowout, Furnessville is closed off now by a new foredune of marram grass, little bluestem and sand cherry.

Cattails grow in an interdunal pond at the eastern edge of Furnessville Blowout.

East of Furnessville, there are more foredunes, obviously much narrower than they once were. They are covered with marram grass, sand reed grass, little bluestem, and sand cherry shrubs, and they are bordered by a strip of jack pines at the edge of a black oak woods.

Big Blowout is wide and shallow, a confused place of rolling hills and valleys much like the west half of Beachhouse Blowout. Jack and white pines climb the slope on the western rim of this blowout. The center is covered with wildflowers, tufts of little bluestem prairie grass, sand cherry and common juniper. The back wall of the blowout is grassy with a few blackened remnants of a "tree graveyard" still standing.

Trail 10 cuts inland not far east of Big Blowout, up a hill

and down a lee slope covered with basswood trees before plunging into another black oak forest, mysteriously labeled "Paradise Valley" by early park officials. Maybe the label just refers to how cool they felt coming in off the hot beach.

High wooded dunes border the trail for awhile on its north side. You can tell when you're adjacent to Big Blowout because two bare sand "slides" lead from its rim down to the trail.

The trail heads west through scattered stands of tall white pines that mingle among the trees of a mixed hardwood forest. Black oaks outnumber the others, but there are also white oaks, sassafras, tulip trees, and sugar maple.

Though this trail passes entirely through upland forest, its route takes it very near the edge of the long marsh that runs the length of the park from east to west. So there are cinnamon ferns, jewelweed, and an occasional skunk cabbage on the low ground south of the path. Virginia creeper and false solomon's seal seem to be everywhere, and there are frequent patches of columbine and wintergreen. (Also known as teaberry, the leaves of wintergreen taste like the chewing gum of that flavor.)

The woods becomes sandier and more open from time to time, as the trail climbs gently onto higher ground. The vegetation is entirely different in these sunnier sections. There are more blueberries usually, more asters and wild grapes.

In the low spots between the hills, the trail passes again through more varied hardwood forest with fewer shrubs and different flowers—more columbine and wintergreen, may apples, baneberry, and once in awhile a jack-in-the-pulpit.

Trail 10 ends at junction with Trails 8 and 9 just north of the long wooden bridge across the marsh that leads to Wilson Shelter.

TRAILS IN THE
NATIONAL LAKESHORE

Description: There are twelve hiking trails or trail systems and one bicycle trail within the National Lakeshore boundaries. Together they total more than 27 miles. However, the trails do not interconnect, and the longest single system—aside from the 9-mile bike trail—is only 5.6 miles long. To get a sense of the park as a whole, you have to sample several of these short paths.

The trail to Mt. Baldy explores the ecology of a wandering dune.

The Ly-Co-Ki-We Horse Trail and the Bailly Homestead Trail are the only footpaths anywhere in dune country that are located on the oldest of all the prehistoric beach ridges, the Glenwood Beach (which is nearly all dense woodland today). The Calumet River Trail is a woodland path that hugs the river bank.

The trail between Chellberg Farm and the Bailly Homestead gives the hiker a glimpse of how human history in the area has affected the landscape.

Trails around Cowles Bog let you investigate swamps and marshes without getting your feet wet. The same trails also wind through an open oak savanna, young by geological standards but one of the oldest dune complexes created by our own Lake Michigan and not by its glacial ancestor, Lake Chicago.

The Calumet Bicycle Trail follows the right-of-way of the Northern Indiana Public Service Company's utility wires. It gives you a chance to see some flowers you won't find in many other places at the dunes, for they are those aggressive plant immigrants from Europe that seem to grow best on disturbed ground—plants like yarrow and Queen Anne's lace and bittersweet nightshade. Despite their bad reputation for driving out native plants, many of them are quite lovely. Red and black raspberries are also abundant in late summer along the bike trail.

The trails at West Beach give the best look at the processes of succession described in this book. You can walk through beaches, foredunes, interdunal ponds, high black oak dunes, and tiny pothole swamps. A trail here also circles Long Lake, the biggest body of open water other than Lake Michigan anywhere in the federal or state park property.

Facilities other than trails in the National Lakeshore include educational exhibits and literature on the dunes available at the Visitors' Center, the beachhouse at West Beach and, soon, at the Paul Douglas Environmental Education Center which will be located at West Beach. The National Lakeshore also offers film and slide programs, interpretive hikes, and field trips directed by park naturalists. There are also four public swimming beaches.

The most heavily developed of the four beaches is West Beach, where a huge beachhouse completed in 1977 provides lockers, showers, toilets, changing rooms, and snack and gift shops. Outdoor picnic facilities are located nearby.

There are parking areas and toilets at the two beaches in Beverly Shores, one at the north end of State Park (Kemil) Road directly north of the National Lakeshore headquarters, and the other at the end of Central Avenue. (Central Avenue runs north from U.S. 12 four miles east of the National Lakeshore headquarters.)

Mount Baldy is 5.3 miles east of the Lakeshore headquarters via U.S. 12 on the Porter/LaPorte County line. A sign on the highway will direct you north on Rice Street to the parking lot. Facilities planned for the beach there include: a well for drinking water, flush toilets, picnic tables, bicycle racks, automobile parking lots, and interpretive natural history exhibits.

National Lakeshore officials ask that visitors refrain from littering and from picking flowers or any other plants unless they have a signed collector's permit, available to researchers under certain conditions from the park headquarters. Berry, nut, and mushroom picking is allowed in moderation. Fires are allowed in the grills provided in formal picnic areas and by permit only elsewhere. (Permits are available at National Lakeshore head-

quarters.) Burning of driftwood or other downed timber is prohibited. The Park Service recommends that you bring your own
charcoal briquets or portable gas stoves.

Dune buggies, motorcycles, and other off-road vehicles are
also prohibited.

The National Lakeshore headquarters is open daily from 8
A.M. to 8 P.M. in summer, 8 A.M. to 6 P.M. spring and fall, and 8
A.M. to 4:30 P.M. in winter. For more information write: Na-
tional Lakeshore Headquarters, R.R. 2, Box 139A, Chesterton,
IN. 46304. Telephone: (219) 926-7561.

Trails in the East Unit

Mount Baldy Trail (½ mile). To reach Mount Baldy, drive
east from the National Lakeshore headquarters 5.3 miles on
U.S. 12 and turn north on Rice Street a few yards east of the
Porter/LaPorte County line. (U.S. 12 makes two right angle
turns just before the Rice Street exit. You should be able to see
the giant bare dune from the highway after the first of these
sharp turns.)

The trail heads northwest from Rice Street up a steep wooded
dune about 100 feet south of the parking lot. Black oak is the
commonest tree. Understory shrubs include witch hazel, sassafras, and shadbush, maple leaf viburnum and hop trees. Brack-
en fern is abundant beside the trail.

The flowers are those found in open black oak dunes near the
beach throughout the area: flowering spurge, blazing star and
goat's rue, horsemint, both common and starry varieties of false
solomon's seal.

The trail splits after a quarter-mile to begin a loop. The
right fork heads northeast for a shortcut onto the open, grassy
foredunes west of the moving dune. The left fork stays longer
in shady woods, continuing northwest to come out on a hill
just above the beach.

The foredunes west of Mount Baldy display a rich assort-
ment of wildflowers. Yellow is predominant—the color of
goldenrods, puccoon, evening primrose, and prickly pear.

The trail from the foredune heads east onto the top of Mount Baldy, a huge mountain of bare sand that is moving inland about four feet a year, too fast, apparently, for vegetation to take root in quantities great enough to halt its progress.

If you look down the slope that faces away from the lake, you may see sprouts of starry false solomon's seal and scattered grapevines, but oaks are still dying as the sand overtakes them.

The windward side of Baldy, sloping down to the lake at a gentler angle, about 15 degrees, is almost completely devoid of vegetation. Bugseed and marram grass huddle near its base. A dark line of humus about halfway up is the only visible sign of a buried forest that will be exposed some day when the dune has moved farther south.

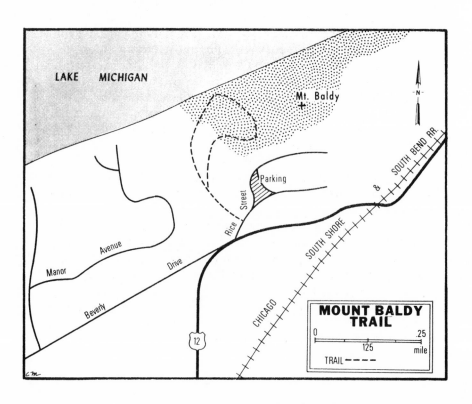

The gray band of sand on the lower beach, the sand that doesn't match the rest in color, was imported by the Army Corps of Engineers to slow the erosion process from recent high lake levels.

Sea rocket, pigweed, bugseed, seaside spurge and marram grass form long defensive lines against the forces of wind and water on the middle and upper beach at Baldy. White gull-feathers cling in summer to the bugseed.

The trail heads west along the beach to join the other fork of the loop at a low spot in a wave-cut cliff on the edge of the woods.

The Bailly Homestead Trail (2.5 miles) offers hikers a glimpse into human as well as natural history of the dunes. The trail route takes you past the early 19th century home, currently being restored, of the area's first settler, Canadian fur trader Joseph Bailly, and also by the cemetery where Bailly and several generations of his descendants are buried.

The path is a wide loop that begins and ends at a parking lot and picnic area on Mineral Springs Road, ¾ mile south of U.S. 12. Mineral Springs Road is 4½ miles west of the National Lakeshore headquarters (1½ miles west of Indiana Route 49, the entrance road to the State Park).

From the parking lot, it heads south first through a forest of giant basswood, beech, and sugar maple trees. It dips into a low, moist woodland carpeted with bloodroot and tooth-wort in late March, woodland phlox and red trillium in late April or early May. It curves west, crosses a wooden bridge and then meanders uphill to emerge in a clearing at the north-east edge of the Bailly Homestead grounds.

Five buildings have been restored or reconstructed on the site of the homestead. The 2½-story main house was begun by Joseph Bailly in 1833 on a hill overlooking the Little Calumet River. It is said that when he arrived in 1822, he tried to build right on the banks of the stream, not yet understanding the concept of a Midwestern flood plain.

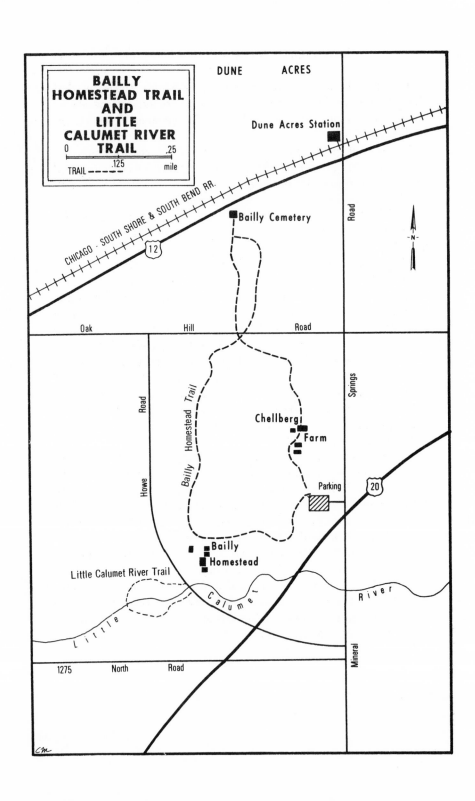

BAILLY
HOMESTEAD TRAIL
AND
LITTLE
CALUMET RIVER
TRAIL

0   .25
          .125
TRAIL ———— mile

DUNE   ACRES

Dune Acres Station

CHICAGO - SOUTH SHORE & SOUTH BEND RR.

12

Bailly Cemetery

Road

-N-

Oak   Hill   Road

Springs

Bailly Homestead Trail

Road

Howe

Chellberg

Farm

Parking

20

Bailly
Homestead

Little Calumet River Trail

Little   Calumet   River

1275   North   Road

Mineral

CM

The house has undergone alterations since Bailly's day, but restorers found the original oak timber intact when they peeled away the white siding. The house passed from family owner-ship following the death of Bailly's granddaughter, Frances Howe, in 1916. It has since been a retreat for Catholic nuns, a restaurant, and a dwelling inhabited by squatters.

A brochure prepared by the National Lakeshore staff iden-tifies the one-story log building adjacent to the house as the chapel. It was a summer kitchen before Rose Bailly, one of the original owner's five daughters, converted it.

The two-story log cabin, referred to by park rangers as a "coachman's house," was at one time a granary, at another time servants' quarters.

A reconstructed log storehouse, across the driveway from the other Homestead buildings, was designed to resemble one Bailly is said to have built for the local Potawatomie Indians who left their furs in his charge while they were away hunt-ing for more game. The going rate for furs in those days was: deerskin, thirty cents; raccoon, sixty-five cents; and wolfskins, one dollar.

The two-story brick house dates from the 1880s, after Joseph Bailly's time. It was originally connected to the main house by a short wooden bridge at the second floor level.

The shaded section of grassy lawn across the road in front of the homestead is covered in spring with red trillium and woodland phlox.

The trail heads north from the homestead through old fields where daisies and black-eyed susans bloom among the crab-apples, hawthorns, and red osier dogwood. Some of these open spaces were lumbered by Bailly's son-in-law, who oper-ated a sawmill.

A row of tall white oaks at the edge of the fields probably marks the route taken by Bailly foot travelers when visiting their neighbors. Farm pigs would have found good natural forage in the acorns at the base of the trees.

When the main trail re-enters the woods and curves east, a side trail splits north to make a half-mile loop that will take you past the Bailly Cemetery. The cemetery is worth the trip even if you have no interest in local history. An elaborate set of raised stone structures, it looks more like a ceremonial altar the Aztecs might have devised than a nineteenth century Christian cemetery.

After the side trail rejoins the main trail, it passes briefly along the edge of a ravine above a wet weather stream. The pink-striped blossoms of spring beauty completely cover the slopes here from late April through mid-May. Hepatica, rue anemone, and yellow violets are scattered among them.

The trail crosses the ravine on a log and heads southeast through a grove of beeches, rare in the dune area, thriving in this moist, sheltered environment along with sugar maples, red oaks, and white ash trees.

It breaks into a clearing, the site of an old farmhouse built on land sold in 1885 by the Bailly son-in-law who ran the sawmill to a former "hired hand," a Swedish immigrant named Chellberg. The farmhouse, made of brick, still looks sturdy. It is surrounded by a wooden barn, maple sugar shed, and various other outbuildings. The National Park Service plans eventually to develop the place as part of its "living history" program, hiring a family to live and recreate on the site the daily activities of Midwest farmers in the early 1900s.

The trail heads south from the farmhouse along an old wagon lane bordered by maple trees to the parking lot and trail's end.

The Little Calumet River Trail is a 2.5-mile loop that connects with the Bailly Homestead Trail at its western end. This trail begins in an elm and ash woods along the banks of the river south of the bridge on Howe Road across from the Bailly Homestead. It follows the south bank of the river closely as it heads west and then crosses the stream on a wooden footbridge and loops north and east back to the Bailly-Chellberg Area.

Along the river bank, the trail traverses forests richer than most in the dunes. Hickories grow here as well as oaks, and along the narrow ravines that carry tributary streams to the river, basswoods, sassafras, and beech are also common. The ravines themselves are excellent places to see spring beauties and other early wildflowers.

After the trail crosses the river, it continues on a boardwalk across a swamp and then climbs into an upland forest. It eventually passes through a stand of red pine—presumably planted by humans—before coming back to the road on the north side of the river.

The Ly-Co-Ki-We Trail (3½ miles) is a loop that begins and ends a mile south of the National Lakeshore headquarters at a parking lot just east of Kemil Road on U.S. 20. The trail's name is said to be a Miami Indian word for sandy ground.

It heads west first through a deep woods of mixed hardwoods on gentle slopes of the oldest glacial beach ridge in

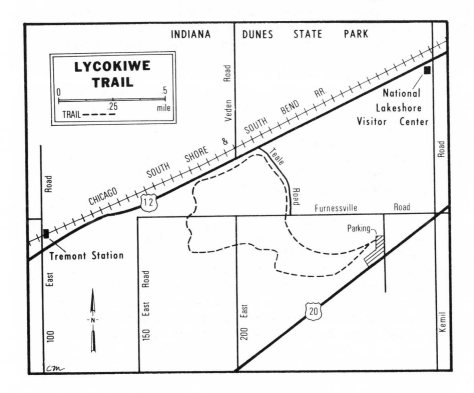

the area, the beach of Lake Chicago's Glenwood stage. Icy water lapped at the shores here some fourteen thousand years ago.

Flowering dogwood is spectacular on this section of the trail in April, blooming just after the parade of tiny, early spring wildflowers—hepatica, bloodroot, spring beauty, and rue anemone.

The trees are black oak, white oak, tulip, sassafras, and sugar maple, a combination that also brings great variety to the fall color in this woods.

In the rich leaf litter at the base of the trees (especially the oak trees), you may find squawroot, a peculiar plant with a thick, scaly, yellow-brown stalk. Unable to manufacture its own chlorophyll to make green leaves, it lives quite well as a harmless parasite on the tree roots.

May apples, spreading by underground runners into patches that seem oddly geometrical, are abundant, too, in the deeply shaded woods. Their flowers, a pale yellow-white, bloom underneath the wide umbrella leaves.

After the trail crosses Veden Road (labeled 200 E. on some maps) it turns north on a wooden footbridge across a marsh blanketed with marsh marigold and swamp buttercup in spring.

The trail comes out then on a 55-acre tract of open grass and scrubland, pocked with the charred trunks of dead trees. The fire occurred in 1971, and since 1973 records of the changes in vegetation and animal life have been kept by a local resident, Mrs. Emma Pitcher, as a research project of the Chicago Audubon Society. Bluebirds appeared for the first time in 1976 to build nests in the holes woodpeckers had carved out in the dead trees.

The trail continues through the burn area north of Furnessville Road and passes over a high beach ridge that dates from the Calumet stage of Lake Chicago, when the lake's elevation was some forty feet higher than Lake Michigan is today. Some of the ridges have become heavily eroded in recent years, possibly a result of greater exposure to wind since fire destroyed their vegetative cover.

A lilac bush perches incongruously atop one of them. No other signs remain of the farmhouse that must once have stood nearby.

The trail turns east in a narrow band of woodland that borders U.S. 12, follows Teale Road south past a row of houses, and crosses Furnessville Road again before plunging back into old mixed hardwood forest. It angles southeast, passes briefly through an overgrown field (full of asters and daisies in summer) and joins the other end of the loop near the parking lot.

The Cowles Bog Trail (5.7 miles total). The Cowles Bog Trail begins at the parking lot by the Dune Acres train stop on the Chicago, South Shore and South Bend Railroad. It's half a block north of U.S. 12 on Mineral Springs Road, 4½ miles west of the National Lakeshore headquarters. This path is called Cowles Bog Trail on National Lakeshore brochures, though it passes no closer than half a mile to the actual bog. A gate blocks the trail at its beginning, and it is open to the public only on guided tours conducted by park rangers, because part of it passes through private property owned by the Northern Indiana Public Service Company.

It follows a dirt road under NIPSCO utility lines west for three-quarters of a mile, briefly on the edge of a swamp forest and then along the southern edge of the Great Marsh. The marsh is part of a narrow wetland band that runs parallel to U.S. 12 through most of the dune country between Gary and Michigan City. It is quite wide here, maybe a third of a mile across, a waving sea of cattails. The clutch of tamaracks you can see off in the distance is part of Cowles Bog. It remains closed to visitors until the National Park Service can find money and time to provide the kind of access that minimizes damage to the fragile ecosystem.

In scattered open ponds on the south side of the trail, you may see horned grebes during spring and fall migration and

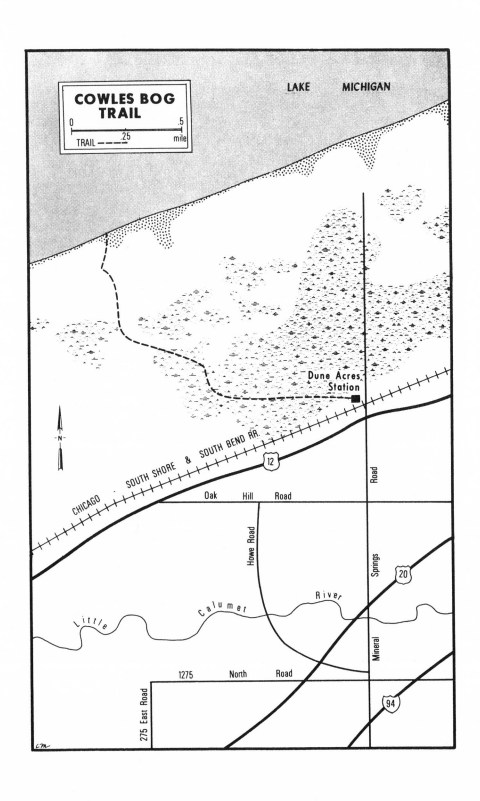

COWLES BOG TRAIL

LAKE   MICHIGAN

0   .5
                    .25
TRAIL ------   mile

Dune Acres
Station

-N-

CHICAGO   SOUTH SHORE   &   SOUTH BEND R.R.

12

Oak   Hill   Road

Howe Road

Road

Springs

20

Little   Calumet   River

Mineral

1275   North   Road

275 East Road

94

diving ducks like buffleheads, goldeneyes, and scaups along with the more familiar mallards. In recent years, a couple of black-crowned night herons have visited one of these ponds on their annual spring trip north.

The trail turns north after three-quarters of a mile, crossing a narrow section of the marsh in a series of right angle turns along a high eastern embankment. Tree swallows build nests in the dead trees of swampy areas along this section of trail, and bullfrogs call out in their deep booming voices from the muddy bottoms.

There are dense thickets of chokeberry, staghorn sumac, and red osier dogwood on the swamp edges. Sourgum trees grow on the pointed end of a wooded peninsula that juts out among the cattails. The pale blue, almost white cleft phlox native to the dunes grows on an open slope among scattered oaks on the west side of this peninsula east of the trail.

After a three-quarter mile walk along the embankment the trail heads east across a ditch into a sandy black oak woods. It proceeds north then across a series of wooded dunes half a mile to the beach. The trees are widely spaced along much of this section, allowing sunlight in to nourish plants like New Jersey tea, goat's rue, fern-leaved false foxglove, and various kinds of blazing star. The blueberries here are the early lowbush type, and they ripen by mid-July.

The beach at the end of the trail is wide and clean, seldom used because it can't be reached by car. The only litter is driftwood. If you bring a lunch, make sure to pack its remains back out with you.

Heron Rookery Trail (1.6 miles). The Heron Rookery is an isolated area added to the National Lakeshore to protect its namesake—a tree-top rookery that provides nesting space to about 40 pairs of great blue herons. The park property is a large block of lowland forest along the Little Calumet River between 450 East Road and 600 East Road about a half mile south of 1400 North Road. The road runs east from U.S. 20 about 1.5 miles east of its junction with Indiana 49.

Great blue herons, while not yet rare enough to make the endangered species list, have declined in numbers due to a loss of wetland feeding areas and nesting habitat in mature lowland forests. They build their nests in dense colonies in the crowns of trees. These stately birds are very temperamental about their nests. If people draw too near, the adults will fly, leaving their downy young to the mercies of sun, rain, and passing crows and their eggs to cold and death. From early spring until late summer, therefore, the Park Service asks everyone to stay away from the North Bank of the Little Calumet River.

Fortunately, the trail is on the south bank. Like many others in the park it was created by feet and not by design so don't be surprised if you get your feet wet. The trail follows the river bank through the forest, and the display of spring wildflowers is excellent.

Unfortunately the river has been channelized, converted to a ditch as straight, uniform, and gently sloped as an interstate highway. Spoil banks mar the scenery in some places. However, the forces that give natural rivers their meandering curves are working on the Little Calumet—a sand bar here, an undercut bank there, and the river will assert itself.

The Calumet Bicycle Trail (9.2 miles) extends from Mineral Springs Road (at the Dune Acres train station of the Chicago, South Shore and South Bend Railroad) northeast in a straight line to the Porter-LaPorte County line near Mount Baldy.

Access points along the way (listed from west to east) are at Waverly Road, Indiana Route 49 (entrance road to the State Park), Tremont Road (a second train stop for the South Shore Railroad), State Park Road (also known as Kemil Road) across U.S. 12 from the National Lakeshore headquarters building, Broadway Street and a second road in Beverly Shores simply labeled 500 E. and Central Avenue. The trail was constructed by the Indiana Department of Natural Resources in cooperation with the National Park Service and Northern Indiana Public Service Company. Its surface is an eight-foot-wide layer of finely ground slag chips. The track was soft and grooved, difficult to navigate in the summer of 1976, its first season. Designers promised it would pack down naturally over the winter. Barriers installed at every road crossing to keep out motorized vehicles are also moderately awkward for travelers without motors. One has to dismount and walk the bicycle through.

The trail passes entirely through sunny fields and along the edges of open marshes, so we recommend hats (and canteens of cold water) on warm days.

The section of trail between Mineral Springs Road and the Tremont train stop is bordered on the north by low marshy areas inhabited by thickets of willow and chokeberry and by patches of moist woodland where oaks, red maples, cottonwoods, and sassafras grow.

Fields on the south side of the trail, stretching away to the railroad tracks, are filled with bunches of narrow-leaved mountain mint, low steeplebush and meadowsweet shrubs, daisies, sunflowers, and purple flowering loosestrife. Marsh ferns grow in the damp ditches along with cattails and occasional clumps of small forget-me-nots. Raspberries, both black and red varieties, are plentiful.

Between Tremont and Kemil Road (about a mile), the land rises south of the trail to make a wall of green and flowering plants in summer. Monarch and swallowtail butterflies skim over the blossoms of milkweed, blue vervain, boneset, and joe pye weed in search of nectar. Cicadas hum constantly, competing with the crackle of the electric lines.

Trees in a forest north of the trail are mainly red maple and black oak.

The section of trail between Kemil Road (eastern boundary of the State Park) and Broadway in Beverly Shores (about 1.4 miles) is open and weedy for the most part, with ragweed among the commonest of plants.

Patches of prairie-like meadow are scattered in between the weeds, however. Blazing star, its low flowering stalks bright purple in midsummer, grows in these patches. So do goldenrods, milkweed, flowering spurge, and horsemint.

As you near Broadway, the land becomes wetter again and cattails reappear. The cattails continue between Broadway and the road labeled 500 E. They are interspersed with wil-

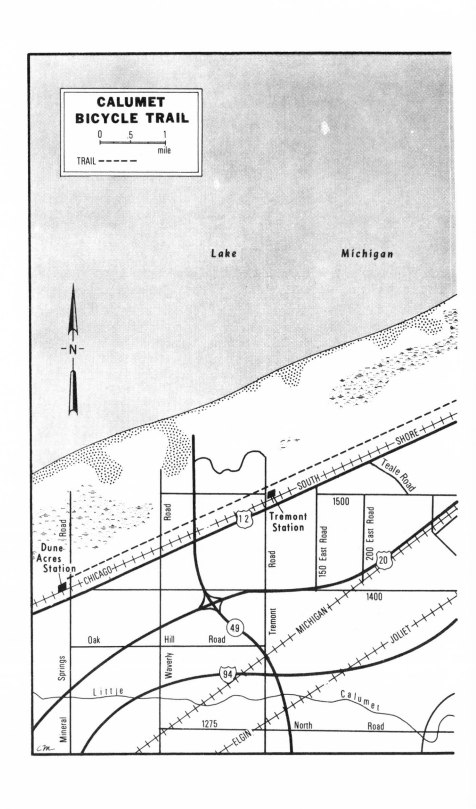

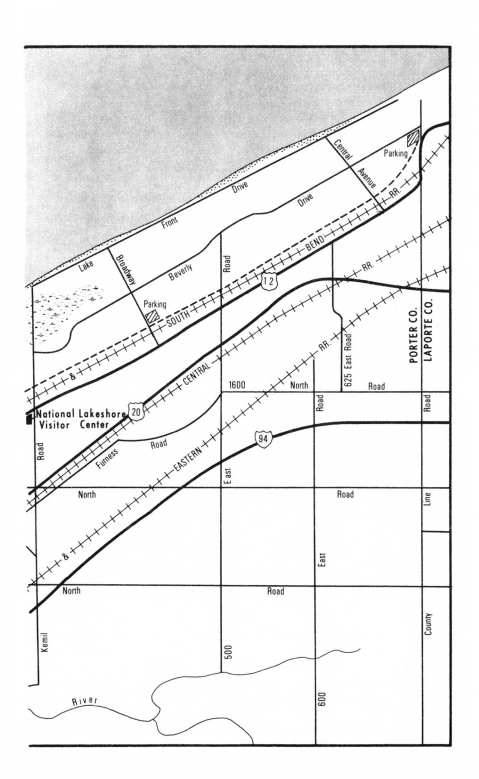

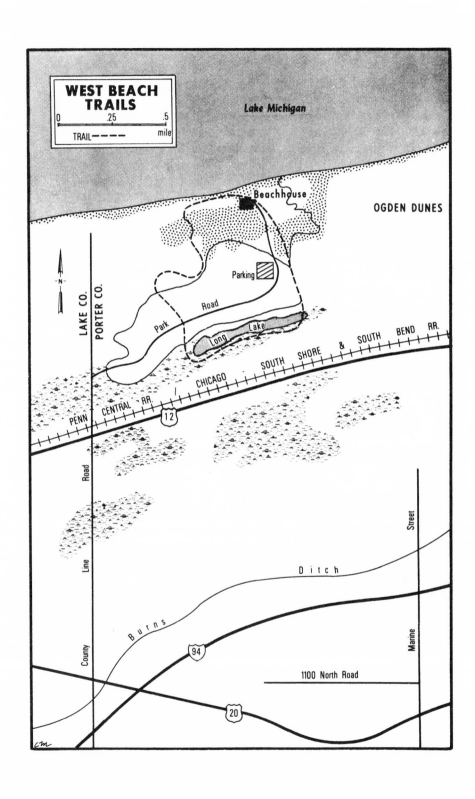

WEST BEACH
TRAILS

0   .25   .5

TRAIL ----   mile

Lake Michigan

Beachhouse

OGDEN DUNES

-N-

LAKE CO.

PORTER CO.

Parking

Park   Road

Long   Lake

CHICAGO   SOUTH   SHORE   &   SOUTH   BEND   RR.

PENN   CENTRAL   RR.

12

Road

Line

County

Burns

Ditch

Street

Marine

94

1100 North Road

20

CM

lows, sedges, and cardinal flowers that bloom bright red in September.

The ground becomes higher and drier again, the fields at trailside covered with goldenrod, daisies, and blazing star, between the 500 E. Road and trail's end just past Central Avenue where U.S. 12 turns north on the county line.

Trails in the West Unit

West Beach Trails. Three interconnecting trails, the West Beach Hiking Trail (1.6 miles), the West Beach Succession Trail (0.9 miles), and the Marquette Trail (1.4 miles) begin at West Beach. Both the hiking and succession trails are in the West Unit fee area where a nominal admission is charged in spring, summer, and autumn.

The **West Beach Hiking Trail** is a loop best started either at the entrance kiosk for the West Beach Area or at the north end of the parking lot. The loop passes through woods rich enough to boast maidenhair fern and follows high dunes where only pioneering marram grass and cottonwood grow. It crosses a flat, sand-mined area now recolonized by dune plants and then traces the northern shore of Long Lake, climbing up over some high dunes that give a good view of the water. Eventually, boardwalks will carry the trail over wet sections of the Long Lake shore, but until that is done, you will have to take to the road for short stretches. This trail also joins the Marquette Trail near the entrance kiosk.

The Marquette Trail runs west from West Beach to Grand Avenue in Gary, currently along an abandoned railroad track. It is a pleasant walk along a rich cattail marsh. You may see ducks in patches of open water and early on a summer morning many marsh birds will be calling. There are oak-bordered dunes along the north side of the route as well.

West Beach Dune Succession Trail (0.9 miles). This trail begins on the beach about 200 yards east of the West Beach Bathhouse. A post set in the sand usually marks the start.

At the water's edge, you can stand on a sloping shelf of wet sand called a berm and perhaps see your first dunes wildlife. Shorebirds—black-bellied plovers, spotted sandpipers, sanderlings—feed here during their spring and fall migrations, and ring-billed or herring gulls might be seen at anytime. Insects include lady bugs, robber flies, and two species of tiger beetles—white and copper—that figured in Victor Shelford's studies of animal succession in the dunes. Just up the beach on the dry sand, you may find bugseed, sea rocket, or other beach annuals.

The beach ends on a sharp break, a wall of sand nearly 6 feet high held in place by dense clusters of marram grass. The interwoven roots of this growth are usually exposed at the slope. The first cottonwoods appear on the lee side of this first dune, and the steep slope of the second dune was shaped by a mature cottonwood with multiple trunks at least 15 feet of which are buried in the sand. Little bluestem and sandreed grass appear for the first time behind the cottonwoods.

The trail continues inland past jack pine stands carpeted with bearberry and interdunal ponds surrounded by Kalm's St. Johnswort, baltic rush, and Kalm's lobelia. Beyond them is a blowout, a huge bowl of bare sand with a tree graveyard, a ghost forest of dead trees once covered over by sand and now exposed along its western edge. The Park Service has built stairs up the ridge of this dune into an oak forest. This trail ends where it joins the West Beach Hiking Trail in the sand-mined area east of the parking lot.

Inland Marsh Trails (4.9 miles). Parking for Inland Marsh is off U.S. 12 about 1.5 miles east of County Line Road. From there, you follow an entrance trail for about two-thirds of a mile until it hooks up with a network of trails. The Park Service says the network is 4.25 miles long, but there are actually more trails than that. These paths have been created by feet, not by landscape architects. They are not marked, so it is easy to get lost in the Inland Marsh if you don't pay attention to where you are going.

The trails primarily follow the high ridges of the Tolleston dunes, which tend northwest-southeast. There are reedy ponds in the low places between the ridges. Marsh wrens and red-wings are common in the reeds, and such rare species as king rail have been heard calling during nesting season.

The upland portions of the Inland Marsh area are mostly oak savanna, and the open nature of the terrain provides some fine views from the ridge tops. Some of these open areas are being heavily colonized by quaking aspen, but there is still much prairie and savanna vegetation. In late May and early June there is a fine display of lupines here.

Trails planned for the Paul H. Douglas Environmental Education Center. When the center is completed, it will serve as the starting and ending point for trails into the Miller Woods area and into the western extremity of the park. Miller Woods is one of the most diverse areas in the park. It includes areas of black oak savanna as well as one of the most complex foredune systems still in existence. Interdunal ponds and a lagoon connected with the Grand Calumet River fill the low areas.

The western extremity of the park includes a section of the Grand Marsh as well as a swell and swale complex of high dunes and low interdunal ponds.

Some of these trails will follow existing footpaths, and access to these may be allowed before the education center is finished. Check at the park Visitors' Center at Kemil Road in the East Unit or at the entrance kiosk to West Beach for current information.

Appendix I
FURTHER READING

Field Guides

Burt, William H., *Mammals of the Great Lakes Region.* Ann Arbor MI: University of Michigan Press, 1957. Illustrations of most common area mammals and excellent range maps complement a text that keeps technical terms to a minimum.

Chicago Audubon Society, *Birds of the Indiana Dunes National Lakeshore.* A checklist of birds keyed by habitat and by time of year you are most likely to see them at the dunes. Species known to breed at the Lakeshore are marked with an asterisk.

Courtenay, Booth, and James H. Zimmerman, *Wildflowers and Weeds* [of the Great Lakes Region]. New York: Van Nostrand Reinhold Co., 1972. Small color illustrations accompany brief descriptions of every plant mentioned. Requires ability to use a taxonomic key.

Hill, John R., *Geology for the Public: A Field Guide to the Lake Michigan Shore in Indiana.* Bloomington: Department of Natural Resources, State of Indiana, 1973. Pamphlet explains in layman's language, with technical terms defined, historical and current processes determining geology of the dunes.

Mohlenbrock, Robert H., *Forest Trees of Illinois.* Springfield: Department of Conservation, Division of Forestry, State of Illinois, 1973. Photographs of tree trunks, line drawings of leaves, buds, and twigs, and state range maps accompany brief descriptions of commonest area trees.

Peattie, Donald Culross. *Flora of the Indiana Dunes.* Chicago: Field Museum of Natural History, 1930. This is the only attempt still in print to present a complete plant list and description geared specifically and solely for the Indiana Dunes area. The material is arranged in taxonomic order and requires some knowledge of botanical terms, along with ability to use a taxonomic key. The main disadvantage is that many of the plants described no longer survive in the area. Small selection of black and white illustrations, and a few maps are included.

Reshkin, Mark, *et al. The Indiana Dunes Story.* Beverly Shores IN: Shirley Heinze Environmental Fund. A collection of articles on natural and human history at the dunes.

Smith, Helen V., *Michigan Wildflowers.* Bloomfield Hills MI: Cranbrook Institute of Science, 1966. A good current selection of common local wildflowers, including 231 black and white illustrations, 17 color plates, and numerous drawings. Requires ability to use a taxonomic key.

Swink, Floyd, and Gerould Wilhelm, *Plants of the Chicago Region,* third edition. Lisle IL: Morton Arboretum, 1979. An exhaustive listing of area flora with common associates of each species in various habitats (including specific mention of the dunes). Local flowering dates are listed for herbaceous species. Alphabetical by Latin names, cross-referencing by English common names. Includes range maps. This book does not attempt plant descriptions, nor is it illustrated.

Gerould Wilhelm has also written a *Report on the Special Vegetation of the Indiana Dunes National Lakeshore,* published by the National Park Service in 1980. This is a very thorough account of the plants that give the dunes its botanical identity. Includes breakdowns of distribution of plant species and habitat types on all the land now in the Indiana Dunes National Lakeshore.

Other Reading

Four other local books, not strictly field guides, are still useful to amateur naturalists because they contain chapters which describe natural features of the dunes area. They are: *The Indiana Dunes,* by Larry Waldron, photographs by Robert Daum (Philadelphia: Eastern Acorn Press); *Doing the Dunes,* by Jean Komaiko and Norma Schaeffer (Beverly Shores IN: Dunes Enterprises); *Reading the Landscape,* by May Theilgaard Watts (New York: Macmillan Co.). *A Naturalist in the Great Lakes Re-*

gion, by Elliott Rowland Downing (Chicago: University of Chicago Press) is out of print but available on library loan.

The long political battle that led to the creation of both the Indiana Dunes State Park and the National Lakeshore is covered in three recent books. Theologian Ronald J. Engel, in *Sacred Sands: The Struggle for Community in the Indiana Dunes* (Middletown, Conn.: Wesleyan University Press, 1983), discusses the Midwestern progressives who made saving the dunes an article in a democratic faith. Kay Franklin and Norma Schaeffer, in *Duel for the Dunes: Land Use Conflict on the Shores of Lake Michigan* (Chicago: University of Illinois Press, 1983), recount the long battle between those who wanted the dunes for industry and those who wanted them preserved as a park. The battle between industry and preservation is part of the story told in *The Indiana Dunes Story: How Nature and People Made a Park,* edited by Glenda Daniel and published by the Shirley Heinze Environmental Fund, 1984. This volume also covers the foundation of the park and the conflicts that have developed over competing uses for park land.

Appendix II
PLANT LIST BY HABITAT

Nature does not always arrange herself in the orderly fashion favored by the writers of books. Blame nature, then, and not us, please, if you find an evening primrose at the edge of a swamp instead of on the foredunes where we say it belongs.

Plants illustrated in the book are marked with an asterisk. Common associates of these plants, not mentioned in the text, or mentioned but not described in detail for lack of space, are enclosed in parentheses.

BEACH

herbaceous

*Ammophila brevigulata	marram grass
*Cakile edentula	sea rocket
*Calamovilfa longifolia	sand reed grass
*Corispermum hyssopifolium	bugseed
*Cycloloma atriplicifolium	winged pigweed
*Elymus canadensis	wild rye
*Euphorbia polygonifolia	seaside spurge
*Xanthium strumarium	cocklebur

FOREDUNES

herbaceous

*Ammophila brevigulata	marram grass
*Andropogon scoparius	little bluestem grass
*Arabis lyrata	sand cress
*Arctostaphylos uva-ursi	bearberry
*Artemisia caudata	wormwood
*Asclepias syriaca	common milkweed
*Asclepias tuberosa	butterfly weed
(Asclepias viridiflora)	green milkweed
*Calamovilfa longifolia	sand reed grass
*Cirsium pitcheri	sand thistle
*Elymus canadensis	wild rye
*Lithospermum croceum	hairy puccoon
*Monarda punctata	horsemint

*Oenothera biennis	evening primrose
*Opuntia humifusa	prickly pear
*Pteridium aquilinum latiusculum	bracken fern
*Smilacina stellata	starry false solomon's seal
Solidago racemosa gillmani	Gillman's goldenrod
*Solidago speciosa	showy goldenrod

shrubs and vines

*Celastrus scandens	bittersweet
*Cornus stolonifera	red osier dogwood
*Prunus pumila	sand cherry
*Ptelea trifoliata	hop tree
*Rhus aromatica	fragrant sumac
*Rhus radicans	poison ivy
*Rosa blanda	early wild rose
*Rosa carolina	pasture rose
*Salix syrticola	dune willow
Vitis aestivalis	summer grape
*Vitis riparia	riverbank grape

trees

*Populus deltoides	cottonwood

BLOWOUTS

herbaceous

*Ammophila brevigulata	marram grass
*Andropogon scoparius	little bluestem grass
*Arctostaphylos uva-ursi	bearberry
*Artemisia caudata	wormwood
*Asclepias syriaca	common milkweed
*Asclepias tuberosa	butterfly weed
(Asclepias viridiflora)	green milkweed
*Calamovilfa longifolia	sand reed grass
*Cirsium pitcheri	sand thistle
*Elymus canadensis	wild rye
*Equisetum hyemale affine	scouring rush
*Euphorbia corollata	flowering spurge
(Hudsonia tomentosa)	false heather
*Lithospermum croceum	hairy puccoon
*Monarda punctata	horsemint
(Panicum villosissimum pseudopubescens)	white-haired panic grass

(Polygonella articulata)   jointweed
*Smilacina stellata   starry false solomon's seal
*Solidago racemosa gillmani   Gillman's goldenrod

shrubs and vines
*Cornus stolonifera   red osier dogwood
*Juniperus communis depressa   common juniper
*Juniperus virginiana crebra   red cedar
*Prunus pumila   sand cherry
*Ptelea trifoliata   hop tree
*Salix glaucophylloides
   glaucophylla   blue-leaved willow
*Salix interior   sandbar willow
*Salix syrticola   dune willow

trees
*Pinus banksiana   jack pine
*Pinus strobus   white pine
*Populus deltoides   cottonwood
*Quercus alba   white oak
*Quercus velutina   black oak

INTERDUNAL PONDS

herbaceous
(Asclepias viridiflora)   short green milkweed
*Aster ptarmicoides   upland white or stiff aster
(Cladium mariscoides)   twig rush
*Gentiana crinita   fringed gentian
*Gerardia purpurea   purple gerardia
*Hypericum kalmianum   Kalm's St. John's wort
*Juncus balticus littoralis   baltic or lakeshore rush
(Linum medium texanum)   small yellow flax
*Lobelia kalmii   Kalm's lobelia
(Lycopus americanus)   water horehound
(Rhynchospora capillacea)   hair beak rush
*Sabatia angularis   rose pink
(Scirpus americanus)   chairmaker's rush
*(Scirpus brachycarpus)   short-fruited rush
(Scirpus validus)   soft-stemmed or great bulrush
Spiranthes cernua   nodding ladies' tresses
*Triglochin maritima   bog arrow grass

Typha angustifolia	narrow-leaved cattail
Typha latifolia	common cattail
*Utricularia cornuta	horned bladderwort

shrubs and vines

*Cornus stolonifera	red osier dogwood
*Prunus pumila	sand cherry
Salix glaucophylloides glaucophylla	blue-leaved willow
Salix interior	sandbar willow
*Salix syrticola	dune willow

trees

*Populus deltoides	cottonwood

EVERGREEN ASSOCIATIONS

herbaceous

*Arctostaphylos uva-ursi	bearberry

shrubs and vines

*Juniperus communis	common juniper
*Juniperus virginiana	red cedar

trees

*Pinus banksiana	jack pine
*Pinus strobus	white pine

BLACK OAK SAVANNAS

herbaceous

*Arctostaphylos uva-ursi	bearberry
*Andropogon scoparius	little bluestem grass
(Anemone cylindrica)	thimbleweed
(Antennaria plantaginifolia)	pussytoes
*Arabis lyrata	sand cress
*Artemisia caudata	wormwood
*Asclepias syriaca	common milkweed
*Asclepias tuberosa	butterfly weed
*Aster azureus	sky blue aster
*Aster linariifolius	flax-leaved aster
*Calamovilfa longifolia	sand reed grass

*Carex pensylvanica — Pennsylvania sedge
Ceanothus americanus — New Jersey tea
(Comandra richardsiana) — bastard toadflax
*Euphorbia corollata — flowering spurge
Gaultheria procumbens — wintergreen
(Gerardia pedicularia) — fern-leaved false foxglove
(Helianthemum canadense) — common rockrose
Helianthus divaricatus — woodland sunflower
*Koeleria cristata — junegrass
(Krigia biflora) — false dandelion
*Lespedeza capitata — round-headed bush clover
Liatris cylindracea — cylindrical blazing star
*Liatris aspera — rough blazing star
*Lithospermum croceum — hairy puccoon
*Lupinus perennis occidentalis — lupine
*Monarda punctata villicaulis — horsemint
*Opuntia humifusa — prickly pear
Panicum virgatum — switch grass
*Phlox bifida — cleft phlox
Phlox divaricata — woodland phlox
(Phlox pilosa) — prairie phlox
*Pteridium aquilinum latiusculum — bracken fern
(Rudbeckia hirta) — black-eyed susan
*Rosa carolina — pasture rose
*Smilacina stellata — starry false solomon's seal
(Solidago caesia) — blue-stemmed goldenrod
(Solidago speciosa) — showy goldenrod
(Stipa spartea) — porcupine grass
(Tephrosia virginiana) — goat's rue
Tradescantia ohiensis — Ohio spiderwort
*Viola pedata — birdsfoot violet

shrubs and vines

*Amelanchier arborea — shadbush
(Amelanchier laevis) — Allegheny shadblow
(Cornus racemosa) — gray dogwood
Gaylussacia baccata — black huckleberry
*Hamamelis virginiana — witch hazel
Prunus pensylvanica — pin cherry
*Prunus virginiana — choke cherry
Rhus aromatica — fragrant sumac
*Rhus copallina — winged sumac
*Rhus radicans — poison ivy
*Vaccinium angustifolium — late lowbush blueberry

*Vaccininium vacillans   early lowbush blueberry

trees
*Quercus alba   white oak
*Quercus velutina   black oak

PRAIRIES

herbaceous
Andropogon gerardi   big bluestem grass or turkey
                                    foot
*Aster linariifolius   flax-leaved aster
(Buchnera americana)   blue hearts
(Cacalia atriplicifolia)   pale Indian plantain
(Castilleja coccinea)   Indian paintbrush
(Eryngium yuccifolium)   rattlesnake master
*Lespedeza capitata   round-headed bush clover
*Liatris aspera   rough blazing star
 Liatris cylindracea   cylindric blazing star
(Spiranthes lacera)   slender ladies' tresses
(Stipa spartea)   porcupine grass

DEEP WOODS

herbaceous
Anemonella thalictroides   rue anemone
Aquilegia canadensis   columbine
Aralia nudicaulis   wild sarsaparilla
Arisaema atrorubens   jack in the pulpit
(Aster macrophyllus)   big-leaved aster
(Aster sagittifolius)   arrow-leaved aster
(Botrychium virginianum)   rattlesnake fern
Claytonia virginica   spring beauty
(Dentaria laciniata)   toothwort
Gaultheria procumbens   wintergreen
Geranium maculatum   wild geranium
Hepatica americana   hepatica
Maianthemum canadensis   Canada mayflower
Medeola virginiana   Indian cucumber root
(Mitchella repens)   partridge berry
Osmorhiza claytoni   hairy sweet cicely
(Osmunda cinnamomea)   cinnamon fern
Podophyllum peltatum   may apple
Polygonatum canaliculatum   solomon's seal

Polygonatum pubescens — downy solomon's seal
(Prenanthes alba) — white lettuce or lion's foot
(Sanguinaria canadensis) — bloodroot
Smilacina racemosa — common false solomon's seal
(Solidago caesia) — blue-stemmed goldenrod
Thalictrum dioicum — early meadow rue
Trillium grandiflorum — large trillium
Trillium recurvatum — red trillium
Uvularia grandiflora — bellwort
Viola papilionacea — common blue violet
Viola pensylvanica — yellow violet

shrubs and vines

*Amelanchier arborea — shadbush
*Euonymus obovata — running strawberry bush
Gaylussacia baccata — huckleberry
*Hamamelis virginiana — witch hazel
*Lindera benzoin — spicebush
Parthenocissus quinquefolia — virginia creeper
*Prunus virginiana — choke cherry
Sambucus canadensis — black-fruited elderberry
Sambucus pubens — red elderberry
*Viburnum acerifolium — maple-leaved viburnum
*Vaccinium angustifolium — late lowbush blueberry
*Vaccinium vacillans — early lowbush blueberry

trees

*Acer saccharum — sugar maple
(Carpinus caroliniana virginiana) — blue beech
(Carya cordiformis) — bitternut hickory
Carya ovata — shagbark hickory
*Cornus florida — flowering dogwood
*Fagus grandifolia — beech
Fraxinus americana — white ash
Liriodendron tulipifera — tulip tree or yellow poplar
(Ostrya virginiana) — ironwood
Prunus serotina — black cherry
*Quercus alba — white oak
Quercus rubrum — red oak
*Quercus velutina — black oak
*Sassafras albidum — sassafras
*Tilia americana — basswood

MARSHES

herbaceous

(Asclepias incarnata)	swamp milkweed
Brasenia schreberi	watershield
Calamagrostis canadensis	bluejoint grass
Carex stricta	marsh sedge
(Dryopteris thelypteris pubescens)	marsh shield fern
(Elodea canadensis)	common waterweed
(Eupatorium maculatum)	spotted joe pye weed
(Eupatorium perfoliatum)	boneset
(Iris virginica shrevei)	blue flag
Lemna minor	small duckweed
(Lycopus americanus)	common water horehound
Lysimachia terrestris	swamp candles
Nuphar advena	spatterdock
Nymphaea tuberosa	white water lily
Polygonum coccineum	marsh smartweed
Pontederia cordata	pickerelweed
(Potamogeton sp.)	pondweed
Sagittaria graminea	grass-leaved arrowhead
Sagittaria latifolia	common arrowhead
(Scirpus americanus)	chairmaker's rush
(Scirpus validus)	soft-stemmed or great bulrush
Sparganium eurycarpum	bur reed
Typha angustifolia	narrow-leaved cattail
Typha latifolia	common cattail
(Utricularia vulgaria)	great bladderwort

shrubs and vines

Cephalanthus occidentalis	buttonbush
*Pyrus melanocarpa	black chokeberry
Salix interior	sandbar willow

SWAMPS

herbaceous

(Aralia nudicaulis)	wild sarsaparilla
*Caltha palustris	marsh marigold
Coptis groenlandica	goldthread
Cornus canadensis	bunchberry
(Dryopteris thelypteris pubescens	marsh shield fern
Impatiens capensis	jewelweed

(Iris virginica shrevei)	blue flag
(Onoclea sensibilis)	sensitive fern
(Osmunda cinnamomea)	cinnamon fern
(Osmunda regalis spectabilis)	royal fern
(Polystichum acrostichoides)	Christmas fern
(Rubus hispidus obovalis)	swamp dewberry
(Saururus cernuus)	lizard's tail
(Smilax rotundifolia)	greenbrier
*Symplocarpus foetidus	skunk cabbage

shrubs and vines

Cephalanthus occidentalis	buttonbush
Gaylussacia baccata	huckleberry
*Pyrus melanocarpa	black chokeberry
*Rhus vernix	poison sumac
Salix interior	sandbar willow

trees

Acer rubrum	red maple
Betula lutea	yellow birch
Nyssa sylvatica	sourgum
Quercus macrocarpa	bur oak
Quercus palustris	pin oak

BOGS

herbaceous

(Calopogon pulchellus)	grass pink
(Cypripedium acaule)	pink lady's slipper
Drosera intermedia	spatulate-leaved sundew
*Drosera rotundifolia	round-leaved sundew
(Dryopteris thelypteris pubescens)	marsh shield fern
(Habenaria ciliaris)	orange-fringed orchid
(Menyanthes trifoliata minor)	bog buckbean
(Osmunda regalis spectabilis)	royal fern
(Parnassia glauca)	grass-of-parnassus
(Pogonia ophioglossoides)	rose pogonia
*Sarracenia purpurea	pitcher plant
Sphagnum sp.	sphagnum moss

shrubs and vines

Andromeda glaucophylla	bog rosemary

Chamaedaphne caliculata angustifolia	leatherleaf
Gaylussacia baccata	huckleberry
*Rhus vernix	poison sumac
*Vaccinium angustifolium	late lowbush blueberry
*Vaccinium vacillans	early lowbush blueberry
*Vaccinium corymbosum	swamp blueberry
Vaccinium macrocarpon	large cranberry bush
Vaccinium oxycoccos	small cranberry bush

trees

Betula pumila	bog birch
*Larix laricina	tamarack
*Pinus strobus	white pine

Index to Animals and Plants

ANIMALS

PLANTS